Hangman's Brae

First Published 2005
By Black & White Publishing Ltd
99 Giles Street, Edinburgh EH6 6BZ

ISBN 1 84502 039 1

A CIP catalogue record for this book is available from the British Library.

Typeset by RefineCatch Limited, Bungay, Suffolk
Printed and bound by Creative Print and Design

Hangman's Brae

True Crime and Punishment in Aberdeen and the North-East

Norman Adams

BLACK & WHITE PUBLISHING

CONTENTS

Also by Norman Adams:

Blood and Granite – True Crime from Aberdeen

The Wee Book of Aberdeen

ACKNOWLEDGEMENTS

Among the many people who have helped me with this new extended edition of *Hangman's Brae* my grateful thanks are due to the following:

The staff of Aberdeen Central Library (Reference and Local Studies), who dealt with my numerous inquiries; Aberdeen and North-East Scotland Family History Society; Aberdeenshire Library Information Service, Oldmeldrum; Inverness Library (Reference Room); The Mitchell Library, Glasgow (General Services Department); National Library of Scotland (Reference Service); University of Aberdeen Historic Collections and librarians and archivists at Banchory, Banff, Forfar, Fraserburgh, Montrose, Nairn and Peterhead.

I am also indebted to Rachel Benvie, Curator, Montrose Museum; Dr David Bertie, Curator of Local History, Aberdeenshire Heritage; Helen Birnie and Sheila Jessiman, St Fergus; James A. Christie; Tina Craig, Deputy Head of the Royal College of Surgeons of England's Library and Information Services, London; Judith Cripps, Aberdeen City Archivist; Chris Croly, Aberdeen City Council Assistant Keeper (Research), Archeological Unit; Fiona Watson, Archivist, NHS, Grampian; Fraserburgh Heritage Society; Graeme Wilson and Margaret Heron at Moray Council's Local Heritage Department, Elgin; and Calum Ross for copy-editing.

My special thanks go out to my son, Norman G. Adams, for his photography, Dr Joyce Miller, a leading authority on Scottish witchcraft, and to Sandy Strachan and Lys and Jim Wyness.

Credit must also go to Aberdeen City Council (Publicity and Promotions Department); Angus Council Cultural Services for providing the photograph of the Montrose branks; David H. Caldwell,

Keeper Scotland and Europe, National Museums of Scotland, Edinburgh, for permission to reproduce the drawing of 'The Maiden'; and Alex F. Young, a fellow chronicler of crime, for the use of William Calcraft's portrait.

INTRODUCTION

Carryin' great loads the Shore up frae,
By Marischal Street and Hangman's Brae.

John Smith (1830)

A street map of Aberdeen is a guide to the dark side of the city's history for we can use it to walk in the footsteps of the hangman. Climb the Gallowgate and you follow the road to the gallows that stood on a high ridge outside the Gallowgate Port. In a gatehouse lodged the officer who was paid to whip offenders. He might even have acted as hangman.

The granite bow of Justice Street, in the north-east corner of the Castlegate, marks the beginning of a road that led to two execution sites. In the early Middle Ages stood the Justice or Thieves' Port, the gate where they spiked the heads of felons and which led to 'Heiding' or Heading Hill, where the king's justiciar held court in ancient times. Criminals were 'heidit' either with a mighty sword or by means of 'The Maiden', a crude version of the guillotine. In the valley between Heading Hill and Castlehill they burned witches. The cleft between the hills is now Commerce Street.

In a later age, the Justice Port was also the start of the winding road to Gallow Hill, now part of Erroll Street and Trinity Cemetery, reached by way of present-day Park Street over the 'Thieves' Brig'. The gibbet on Gallowgatehill, the city's earliest known hanging site, was shifted to this lonely spot due to the growth of the town. Because of its proximity to Pittodrie Stadium, the breezy, grassy-topped eminence provided a free, if less than panoramic, view of the football ground and was

ix

known by older generations of Dons fans as 'Miser's Hillie' as folk could watch games without having to pay to get in. 'The Gallow Hill' and 'The Gibbett' are clearly identified on Parson James Gordon of Rothiemay's plan of the burgh in 1661. In the next century culprits were hanged and their bodies suspended in iron frames on the 'gibbett' until they were either stolen by anatomists or crumbled to dust. At nearby Footdee, pirates met their fate on hurriedly erected gibbets at the blockhouse.

Hangings occurred at the Ruthrieston crossroads and at Tillydrone, where the Old Aberdeen 'hangie' officiated. A Jacobite spy, Daniel Campbell, was hanged by Redcoats from a tree at the Brig o' Balgownie in 1746. A paper broadcasting his offence was pinned to his chest.

The theatre of punishment in Aberdeen in the eighteenth and nineteenth centuries was the Castlegate. The gallows occupied three sites. After a stubborn Alexander Morison, the last criminal to be gibbeted on Gallow Hill, failed to 'jouk the jibbet' in 1776, executions were switched to the 'Market Place', the causeway opposite King Street. William Webster was the last felon to suffer at this spot. The gallows-stone, which had a socket for the upright post, was unearthed during excavations for the building of public toilets. A stone of the same description was dug up, and reburied, by workmen lifting the tram-lines in 1958. In June 1788 a new-style scaffold was built for the first execution at the door of the tolbooth, directly opposite to Marischal Street, giving rise to a grim jest that ne'er-do-wells would end their days 'facing doon Marischal Street'. Kate Humphrey murdered her husband in 1830. Her husband had prophesised it would be her last view of the world, even if he did not live to see his prophecy fulfilled. Fenton Wyness, architect and noted local historian, arranged for a marker to be set in the 'cassies' at the entrance to Lodge Walk but it vanished during road improvements. A sharp-eyed schoolboy reported its disappearance and it was restored. In the nineteenth century, the condemned walked out of a window in the old town house and on to the scaffold.

Wild Speyside moorland to the east of Elgin was the scene of two murders and a robbery. In an attempt to curb serious crime the culprits were hanged then exhibited in chains at the place where they committed the deed. Elgin, Forfar and Montrose followed the example of Aberdeen and other burghs by erecting a scaffold at the local tolbooth, which served as a jail and townhouse. The Aberdeen high tolbooth – a prison tower, with eighty-six stairs and a steeple – has survived and is now a museum. The laigh (low) tolbooth, which housed the courtroom and civic offices, was replaced with the present municipal buildings. A summerhouse at Duthie Park was built of stones from the laigh tolbooth. Visitors to it would lounge on benches salvaged from the burgh court as model yachts raced across the boating pond in front of them.

Stonehaven's quayside tolbooth, originally a storehouse, became a prison and courthouse in 1600. The town's oldest building now has a museum downstairs and a restaurant above.

You'll find no trace of 'Hangman's Brae' on an Aberdeen street map, nor the fragrant mignonette, which once flowered there. Hangman's Brae was the colloquial term for a steep, narrow, walled path, paved with blue-hued stones, which began in the south-east corner of the Castlegate before plunging towards Virginia Street. The steps opposite to present-day James Street are roughly on a line with the brae, which was originally Futtie Wynd and later known as Castle Brae. The public hangman, the notorious Johnny Milne, lived in the vicinity. The brae led to his home, dubbed 'Hangman's Hoose', on the east bank of the old canal, which was crossed by 'Hangman's Brig', replaced by the 'Tarrie Brig'. The steep hill, a popular, if dangerous, playground during Victorian winters, vanished in 1857 when it was absorbed by a new road, Castle Terrace. A sketch shows 'Hangman's Brae' before its demise. A sign, depicting a matchstick figure on a gibbet, may have advertised a tavern.

Aberdeen's gruesome past continues to fascinate people of all ages. In August 2004 the staff of a city bookshop organised a charity Murder Walk for its customers and over the Christmas period the city council promoted the darker side of the Castlegate's past, with guided tours of the tolbooth. Johnny Milne even made an appearance. The tour ended with a glass of mulled wine in a nearby hostelry which was appropriate for, after nineteenth-century executions, councillors adjourned to the nearby Lemon Tree for a dram to soothe their nerves.

1

WAGES OF BLOOD

A public executioner had one of the foulest jobs in history – but somebody had to do it. So when the post of official hangman in Aberdeen
became vacant in 1805, the year the Aberdeen to Port Elphinstone canal
was opened, the town council placed an advertisement in the *Aberdeen
Journal*, owned by James Chalmers, the founder's son. It read:

> WANTED.
> AN EXECUTIONER FOR the CITY of ABERDEEN.
> Such persons as may wish to be appointed to that Office,
> are desired immediately to apply to George Turriff,
> Dean of Guild's Officer, who will give information
> respecting the Salary and Emoluments of the office,
> which are considerable, besides a Free House.

The vacancy arose after the previous hangman, Jock McDonald, who
was appointed in 1803–04, died in March 1805, without carrying out an
execution. Despite a good salary, the offer of a free house and perquisites,
which included, on market day, a fish out of every creel, a ladleful of
meal from every sack and a peat from every cartload, there was no rush
of applicants.

The vile work of carrying out the law's ultimate sanction was handed
over to coarse and brutal criminals who took up the job with the sole
aim of 'cheating the widdie' – escaping the gallows rope – and collecting
'blood money'. The hangman was a familiar figure who carried out

menial tasks when not hanging or whipping culprits. He was both feared and hated, so he had good reason to look over his shoulder.

Aberdeen was not alone in advertising for a hangman. In 1785, Elgin hoped to tempt a new executioner with a promise of a free house, two acres of land, a number of attractive perks and a considerable salary. But Jock McDonald's successor was eventually found and in Robert Seaton's painting of Castle Street, in 1806, the newly appointed Aberdeen hangman, Johnny Milne, is shown in the foreground selecting one of his 'perks' from a fishwife. Hands that found grimmer work are seen clutching a fat fish. He presents a squat, unkempt figure in a blue greatcoat with a walking stick, perhaps his staff of office, hooked over his arm. A blue Tam o' Shanter bonnet with a red 'toorie' is pulled down over his straggly grey locks. His unwanted presence has not escaped the baleful attention of the fishwives, one of whom is smoking a pipe.

Johnny had worked as a farm labourer and drystone dyker around Aberdeenshire but in April 1806 was convicted of stealing beehives at Corse on Donside. He was said to have worked at the farm of Tillyskukie (Gaelic for 'Hill of the Clumsy Shape') when he committed the offence. He was sentenced to seven years' transportation but, because of the difficulty in finding McDonald's replacement, they offered Johnny the job. He was paid £7 10s for a half-year's salary to 1 October 1806 and he and his family settled in right fine at the 'Hangman's Hoose'. His fearsome wife, Christian Waters, however, was said to be the real head of the household and would resort to blows if her hen-pecked husband stepped out of line. It was little wonder that Johnny took to drink.

After being appointed to his new position, Johnny visited his old haunts around Tillyskukie. He had a nasty streak and, when he tried to get lodgings for the night at Tillyorn, the neighbouring farm, he was shown the door. Fearful the hangman would seek revenge by setting fire to farm buildings, the local farmers kept watch till dawn.

Johnny Milne's first execution was almost his last. The culprit was stoutly-built Andrew Hosack (56), caught red-handed after robbing a cottage at Rubislaw, Aberdeen, in August 1809. Hosack had gained entry by the chimney but a watchdog alerted neighbours. When he was tried at the High Court of Justiciary in April 1810, he appeared under his assumed name of Fraser. He was found guilty of housebreaking and theft and sentenced to hang on 15 June. Sinister rumours swept Aberdeen that

Hosack had been involved in the brutal murders of an elderly George Milne and his daughter Margaret in their home at Upper Auchinachie, near Keith, in January 1797. They had been mangled with an axe and their cottage ransacked and torched. A reward of 100 guineas failed to find their killer or killers. On the eve of his execution, he signed a statement declaring his innocence of the 'horrid murder'. On the scaffold he adhered to it before dying penitently.

But the grim occasion had elements of farce. It was arranged that Hosack's body be carted to the Gallow Hill for burial but every effort by the local authorities to hire a conveyance was thwarted. Attempts were made to secure transport from coalmen on the quay but these failed. It seemed no one was willing to lend or hire out a cart or horse to carry its macabre load. Johnny Milne's white pony, which had grazing around St Clement's Kirkyard, and his cart were 'borrowed', despite his daughter's game efforts to stop the seizure. Johnny was still on the scaffold when he heard how his daughter had been manhandled as she tried to prevent the hijacking of her father's property. The indignant hangman resigned on the spot. The crowd cheered his decision. Hosack was buried in a shallow grave on the Gallow Hill, where his body was promptly stolen that night by medical students. By then Johnny had second thoughts about his 'one-man strike' and was persuaded to carry on as public hangman. No doubt Mrs Milne added weight to her argument.

One of the perks of a hangman's job was to acquire the clothes of the deceased criminal. But after Johnny hanged murderer Mrs Margaret Shuttleworth, in a fierce rainstorm at Montrose in 1821, he declined to accept her saturated attire, remarking, 'She'll be caul' enough even wi' her claise, so let her tak' them.' A new scaffold had been erected outside the town's jail, at a cost of £30, and the hangman's fee was set at £10. A petition for clemency and doubts about her guilt led to a brief respite. After the execution was postponed, Johnny was paid £2 expenses and escorted as far as St Cyrus on the road back to Aberdeen. He returned to finish the job and was paid the balance due to him.

While in Montrose, people were anxious to meet him for the town had no resident executioner. It was noted that 'many persons waited on him at his lodgings; and if his visitors were not as fashionably dressed, his levee was nearly as numerously attended as if he had been Prime Minister'. Despite jibes that only the lower classes attended executions, an Aberdeenshire laird, John Gordon of Craigmyle, 'a most benevolent and kind-hearted man', had a mania for attending Aberdeen hangings and would even be invited on to the scaffold platform.

Johnny Milne's wife strayed to the wrong side of the law after her husband's death. In less than a year, she appeared three times in Aberdeen Police Court on charges of breaking the peace at her former home. In October 1831 the *Aberdeen Journal* tersely reported:

> Christian Waters, or Milne, relict of the late hangman, was once more brought before the Police Court on Wednesday charged with committing a breach of the peace at Hangman's Brae, and breaking a pane of glass in the house of her husband's successor. She was sent 60 days to Bridewell.

The same punishment had been handed out after her previous offences. The reason for Christian's tantrums is unclear but she probably had a grudge against the new hangman or his employers. Johnny Milne's successor was John Scott, a former assistant executioner in Edinburgh.

Johnny Milne's exploits are legendary but a previous hangman, Robert Welsh, held the office for longer. In 1770–71, an anonymous executioner was paid 6s 8d per month and fifteen shillings a year, representing the rent of a house that went with the job. These sums were paid by the Burgh Treasurer and the Dean of Guild forked out an extra £2 14s clothing allowance. Immediately following his appointment on 30 December 1773, the council agreed to increase Welsh's salary to 13s 4d per month. By 1800 this had risen to one guinea (£1 1s) and seven pence. He was still in office in 1800–01 when his total emolument was £12 7s.

The last man to be hanged by him was a brother of the celebrated gypsy robber, Peter Young. John Young stabbed a member of his gang to death at Chapel of Garioch, near Inverurie, but, despite extenuating circumstances, he was sentenced to hang. A plot to free Young from the tolbooth was foiled and the culprit faced Welsh on 11 December 1801. There was a custom in Aberdeen for the hangman to dress the condemned man in his grave clothes but, when Welsh approached, Young shrunk from his grasp, saying, 'I dinna like to hae that creature Robbie Welsh's hands aboot me.' A minister who had shown much kindness dressed Young in his shroud. Young recovered sufficiently enough to offer a town sergeant, who was near collapse, the glass of wine which was meant to fortify the condemned man. (A town sergeant dropped dead at the hanging of murderer Thomas Stewart in 1770.)

Welsh also hired himself out to towns that did not have their own hangmen. On 19 March 1785, he hanged Andrew Low (20), convicted of theft by housebreaking, from the gibbet on the west hip of Balmashanner Hill, on the outskirts of Forfar. Low, a thief from the age of nine, sat on his coffin on the final journey from the tolbooth door in a horse-drawn cart he shared with the minister and the hangman. After Welsh adjusted the noose and Low's bonds and nightcap, which hid his facial contortions, he drove off the horse, leaving the culprit suspended in midair.

Johnny and his brethren carried out their grim work unmasked but in previous centuries the burgh hangman was a man of mystery. When Aberdeen town council met on 18 February 1596, they were forced to admit that 'enorme (horrid) persons, malefactouris, theiffes and res-settaris' had gone unpunished for too long because there was no one suitable to enforce death, banishment, whipping, burning or torture. No sooner was a suitable candidate recruited than townsfolk 'of the meanest and simplest sort' hounded him from the burgh, hurling insults (the term 'hangman' was anathema to the council!) and stones, causing him injury and his employer extreme embarrassment.

The new executioner was John Justice and he was made of sterner stuff than his predecessors because he was still in office the following year when he played a bloody role in the execution of more than a score of witches in Aberdeen. His name was probably a pseudonym and he may have worn a mask when carrying out his grim work. Justice occupied 'the little hous under the tolbuyth stair'. It would appear his dwelling was in a state of disrepair for the council agreed to mend the door and provide a new lock. A proclamation at the Mercat Cross warned that any person, no matter their sex or age, who forced the new hangman to quit by offending him, by word or deed, would be severely punished.

In John Justice's time the common hangman was colloquially referred to as the 'burreour', 'basar' or 'burrio' throughout Scotland. In a later age he was the 'lockman' in Edinburgh (a lock was a measure of meal, which was a perk), the 'staffman' in Stirling (a staff was his insignia of office) and the 'hangie' in Aberdeen.

In an effort to fight disease, the Aberdeen Council in 1578 ordered the 'commoune burreour' to slaughter swine being reared by townsfolk or found roaming the streets or common ground and to sell the carcases, no doubt to swell the council coffers. People were encouraged to take part in the cull. In Banff in 1714, the hangman's other duties included sweeping dung from the streets and preventing dogs from disturbing church services on a Sunday. He was given the power to destroy dogs and was paid forty pennies for each skin. He also wore a special uniform on market days and holidays. Old Aberdeen hangman Archibald Bishop barred dogs from the kirk, which he also cleaned.

Johnny Milne stole beehives and Edinburgh's 'Jock Heich', real name John High, pilfered poultry. A prisoner in Banff Jail, Robert Young, volunteered to be burgh executioner in 1725 and his duties, other than compulsory attendance at court hearings and carrying out various statutory punishments, included sweeping streets, banishing beggars (but not those who were infirm or blind) and ensuring no dogs entered the church on the Sabbath. Young, a vagabond tinker, had little choice in landing his new job for he took up the appointment 'under paine of death' – an arrangement that gives a new meaning to the term 'tied job'.

In January 1728 John Cameron, a horse thief, was released from jail, on the recommendation of Colonel William Grant of Ballindalloch, to become Banff's hangman for life, or face dire consequences. But he served as executioner for only a short time for, two years later, William Cruickshank, of Waterside of Glass, on being convicted of several offences, 'bound himself to serve the burgh in station of a servant and executioner during all the days of his lifetime and that he shall not desert the said service, under pain of being banished from the kingdom and prosecuted for his crimes'. One of Cruickshank's first duties was to go to Aberdeen to execute a criminal. He was escorted by a guard of four men to ensure he did not desert. He was advanced £17 8s. By 1731, a year later, Cruickshank was no longer in office. Alexander Panton, a chapman from Turriff, was appointed executioner with the proviso that, should he desert or withdraw from the town without leave, the magistrates had the power to sentence him to death.

The wages of blood led some rogues to abandon their shady past. At Banff in September 1637, Willie Watt, scourger, hangman and dempster (he pronounced the sentence of doom at the gallows), hanged Francis Brown, 'ane boy of ane evill lyiff', for theft, after passing sentence. Watt's annual salary of £13 6s 8d was paid on Whitsunday. Banff hangman Arthur Kellie's wage was 6s 8d a month when he was appointed in 1653. His perks were half a peck of meal every week, one peck from every load sold on market day and one haddock or whiting out of each basket of fish landed at the port. In 1697, the Banff hangman, Brown, was paid £19 12s, representing sixteen weeks' wages at twelve shillings a week and a pair of shoes costing fifteen shillings. Murieson, his successor, was paid twenty-six weeks' wages of £15 12s, with new shoes costing 13s 4d. After one hanging, his expenses covered the cost of ale, loaves, a rope for scourging the felon and nailing his ear to the cuckstool (the pillory).

When Margaret McKean was hanged at Banff in 1695, the sum of 8s was paid for four fathoms (a measure) of rope to the hangman, plus 2s for small 'towes' to hang her. The total cost of supplying the wood to make the gallows' ladder was sixteen shillings. In 1730, William Cruickshank, the converted criminal, received the following emoluments: a salary, a rent-free house, a new coat every two years and a pair of shoes and stockings annually. In 1744, a successor received a free coat and breeches. His uniform was tailored in Banff from cloth and thread sent by carriage from nearby Turriff. The total cost of labour, materials and transportation was £7 7s 7d.

The small Banffshire coastal town of Cullen had its own executioner. On 28 August 1675, Andrew Wilson was appointed official hangman to Lord Findlater and the town. His perks were one fish out of every fishing boat for every day it went to sea, £30 out of the common good fund to buy a suit of clothes once a year and one peat and a piece of firewood out of every load of peat and fir sold in Cullen. Two years later, the hangman's salary was £6 13s. The town's population in 1694 was 806.

But some hangman found it hard to keep out of trouble. In 1696, George Cobban lost the hangman's job at Cullen after being arraigned for theft of a 'wedder' (ram) and being implicated in other petty crimes. The charge was not proven but, because of his reputation, he was banished from the burgh, under pain of death if he returned. As an additional punishment, he was whipped through the streets of Banff by their hangman. His last official act was to hang a man on the gibbet at Clunehill, Deskford, for stealing a cow. The thief's skull and bones were unearthed by Banff historian William Cramond in 1887, at which time the stones supporting the gibbet could still be seen.

In 1700, Cobban's shoes were filled by George Milne, a thief from Keith. He was convicted of stealing a peck of 'shilling', the grain removed from the husk, from the Laird of Glengerrack's mill. The sheriff decided his crime deserved death or, as the legendary eighteenth-century Scots judge Lord Braxfield might have said, 'Ye wad be nane the waur o' a hangin' but he relented on condition Milne undertook the office of 'marshall' in Cullen.

A gallows was erected on a hill at Dunnottar on the outskirts of Stonehaven around 1600 when the county court moved seawards from the old royal burgh of Kincardine, near Fettercairn. Once the playground of the ancient Scottish kings, little now remains of the old town, apart from a tiny burial ground with a single tombstone. On the 5 November 1700, the sheriff depute of the county, James Keith, appointed a new executioner thus:

> The said day, compeared (appeared before court) John Weir alias Sutherland, son to the deceased George Weir alias Sutherland, sometime at Sutherland Bridge at Caithness. And enacted, bound and obliged him, and hereby enacts and obliges him that he shall officiate and discharge the office of common executioner, hangman, and scourger, within the Sheriffdom of Kincardine, during all the days of his lifetime, and shall live and behave himself honestly, leally (loyally) and truly, during the space foresaid, he always getting and receiving from the said Sheriff-Depute, a peck of meal, or the price thereof, each week during the said space, with an acknowledgement such as the Sheriff pleases for each man that shall happen to be execute and put to death, with a house to live in, and the hangman's croft or the meal thereof in case he do not dwell thereon.
>
> Likeas (also) he grants the receipt of a pot, crook, pair bowells (wooden bowls), pair of tongs, two chests, bassie (large wooden basin or bowl), cap (wooden cup or bowl) etc. In like manner the said John Weir obliges him to the performance of the hail premises under pain of the highest corporal punishment the Sheriff shall inflict upon him, in case of failure.

It was not unknown for members of the same family to inherit the office of hangman (in the last century there were the Pierrepoints and Billingtons) and it is possible that John Weir followed in the footsteps of his father as hangman of Stonehaven.

James, Robbie Welsh's son would also earn his living with his hands and, although he lived near the foot of Hangman's Brae, he did not inherit the gallows. The pious James Welsh was a highly skilled stone-cutter and woodcarver who crafted the votive sailing ships, which would hang in Aberdeen churches. His model of the *Agnes Oswald*, dedicated to the minister's daughter in 1830, can be seen in Denburn Parish Church. 'The hangman's chair', which was carved by James and purportedly used by his father, was in everyday use in an office in Aberdeen town house. A red-padded Queen-Anne-style chair in the St Nicholas room, the old council chamber, is erroneously said to be the executioner's chair.

By the middle of the nineteenth century, the expense of retaining a public hangman was seen as a waste of money by some local authorities. In accordance with the new Burgh Reform Act of 1833, the first moves were made by Aberdeen Town Council to abolish the post and sell the hangman's house by public roup. A council meeting heard that it would be much cheaper to hire one from elsewhere and the office of Aberdeen public hangman was abolished on 27 January 1834. Six months later, Johnny Milne's successor, John Scott, was appointed hangman of Edinburgh, after the bungling John Williams, whose father had executed mass murderer William Burke, quit after only four months in the post. The ill-fated Scott, of whom we shall hear more, would become the last executioner in Scotland to be employed directly by a council.

After Scott departed, Aberdeen was the scene of four public executions. Before he retired, London hangman William Calcraft acted as a 'freelance' executioner and was kept busy in Scotland, as local hangmen became redundant or died. As well as officiating at three executions in Aberdeen, Calcraft hanged criminals in Ayr, Cupar, Dumfries, Edinburgh, Glasgow, Greenlaw, Linlithgow, Montrose, Paisley and Perth. His fee was usually £20 plus expenses. He sold pieces of the rope at five shillings to one pound an inch, the price depending on the notoriety of the felon. In Glasgow a crowd of 100,000 watched as he dispatched Dr Edward Pritchard, the 'prince of poisoners', who, in 1865, became the last man to be publicly hanged in Glasgow.

In September 1865, the schooner *Nymph* was on passage from Montrose to London when seaman Andrew Brown (25), killed Captain John Greig with an axe. After a shipmate, Pert, disarmed him and threw the axe overboard, Brown described himself as 'going stark mad, out of his mind'. Brown steered the vessel to Stonehaven where his mother stayed and where he was apprehended. His plea of insanity was ignored at his trial in Edinburgh and he was sentenced to hang in Montrose, much to the disgust of the townsfolk who felt the execution should have taken place at Stonehaven. On the morning of his execution, 31 January 1866, Brown was taken by special train from Forfar jail to Montrose, where he was hanged by Calcraft on a scaffold outside the former police office in George Street. It was the last execution to be held in Montrose.

At Aberdeen Central Library's local reference department, there is a facsimile of a letter by William Calcraft to an Aberdeen man who applied for the post of governor of the city's East and West (Bridewell) Prisons on 29 June 1862. Nine days earlier Mr A.W. Chalmers, governor of both jails for thirty-seven years, had drowned in a bathing accident at the beach. The applicant, John Jamieson, appended the copy of the hangman's letter, explaining:

> Anxious at all times to promote the happiness and save the pockets of my townsmen I would on any emergency undertake the chaplain's duty and minister to the unhappy burglar. I would not have any scruples to appear on the drop in the event of Calcraft's indisposition on prison engagements and would undertake to perform the last offices of the law with neatness and dispatch.

Calcraft, who had sold pies to the crowds round the Newgate scaffold before becoming a hangman, date-lined his inexpertly written letter, 'Nugeat Prisn, Joon 1862'. It read:

> My Dere sur. I nivir sed to you I wood give up my purfeshun. i am not to purmit my frends to run aweigh with that noshun and prig my sallurium. My karactur is as good as yours or as evin it was i have a Deesided objekshun to travl so far north on akount of my edge (age) and infirmaries but wen you visit London next a few lessons from me wood put you spiff (smart). Nothink mutch to pik up except about the

knot you no that a veri simple afare too. Pluk also is usefool. Pluk goes a grate way only I nose you niver wanted that. Pluk of cours means bran. My idear is you are well kwallyfied and I shood be hapi to doo you too a turn. Egskuse the remark. Make any use of this letter. No more at present. Yours to command. John William Calcraft.

Jamieson, who probably met Calcraft on the executioner's previous visits to Aberdeen, made indiscreet comments to the prison commissioners about Alexander C. Matthews, surgeon, claiming he was actively canvassing for the governor's post because of his experience of prison discipline when he 'spent a portion of his early life (not exceeding sixty days)' in jail. As a young medical student in 1827, Matthews was locked up for one month and fined £20 for bodysnatching at Chapel of Stoneywood, near Aberdeen.

Neither applicant was successful. John Rutledge, a native of Elgin, succeeded the late Mr Chalmers.

2
TALES OF THE SCAFFOLD

Among the sights of Aberdeen in the sixteenth century were the impaled heads of criminals fixed on iron spikes above the Justice Port. At that time, executions were effected by a headsman wielding a two-handed sword on nearby Heading Hill.

In 1574, John Ewyne (Ewen), a burgess of Aberdeen, was convicted of coining and was half-hanged then 'heidit' with a sword. Three years later Adam Donaldson had his head lopped off for killing John Tawse, a sawyer, and Thomas Wright, a servant of Lord Forbes, was beheaded on 28 May 1579 for slaying the Laird of Gartly's servant.

In 1586, John Green and three women, one of whom was his wife, were convicted of poisoning a child 'begotten in adultery'. Green was hanged and quartered and his head spiked on the Justice Port but the others were publicly drowned in 'the Pottie' (a deep pool) at the Quayhead, at the foot of present-day Shore Brae. Drowning was also reserved for Elspeth Mitchell, wife of a burgess, Patrick Maver, for child murder, and murderer Alexander Blyndcele, whose antecedents were members of a rich and influential family, including Robert Blinseile of Pitmuckston, Provost of Aberdeen in 1482.

Beheading by axe or sword proved a messy and horrific affair when left to an inexperienced executioner. So, when the headsman's sword became redundant, 'kissing the maiden' became a euphemism for beheading by 'the Maiden', a crude decapitating machine which was used for the first time in Edinburgh in 1566 and introduced in Aberdeen at a later date. The future Regent of Scotland, James Douglas, Earl of

Morton, is credited with the introduction of the machine in Scotland after seeing the Halifax Gibbet, a similar apparatus, in operation on his travels.

Mary, Queen of Scots became enmeshed in its bloody history when her faithful Italian secretary David Riccio was brutally murdered in the Palace of Holyroodhouse on 9 March 1566. Less than a month later, one of his murderers, Tom Scott, under-sheriff of Perth, became the first person to 'blood' the Maiden's steel. The Edinburgh 'Pynouris' – porters and labourers who also operated in Aberdeen and Perth – were paid seven shillings to transport the Maiden to and from Blackfriars to the Cross in the High Street.

Its grim, gallows-shaped frame, charged with a cruel blade of iron and steel, looms over visitors to the National Museum of Scotland in Edinburgh. At first glance, the oak structure resembles a ten-foot high artist's easel. Copper-lined grooves on the inner faces of the uprights were kept greased to ensure the smooth descent of the axe, sharpened at its edge and weighted at the top with a block of lead.

In his brief history of the Maiden, William McCulloch (1815–69), the keeper of the Museum of Antiquities in Edinburgh, states his belief that the Edinburgh machine was the only one of its kind in Scotland. But, although the Aberdeen Maiden no longer exists, its axe can be seen in the city's Museum of Civic History – and it is almost certain its design was based on its Edinburgh counterpart.

A loyal servant of the James VI, George Keith, the Earl Marischal, a supporter of the reformed kirk and founder of the Marischal College, might have influenced the arrival of the machine. After all, it was stored for safe-keeping at his home in the Castlegate and the king visited the burgh around the time of a double execution. Douglas and Litster were two criminals who were executed. According to the burgh treasurer's accounts of 1594/95, George Annand was hired to convey the machine to Heading Hill and back again to the Earl Marischal's lodging in the Castlegate, where it was kept in the courtyard. His payment of twenty-five shillings included repairs to the machine, sharpening the blade of the axe and lubricating the suspension rope. The particular item reads, 'For ane garrone (a spike) to the madin, mending of her be (by) George Annand, wright, scharping the aix, for saip to the tow, kareing of hir to the hill, and hame agane, to my Lord Merschells cloiss – 25s.' He also received additional payments of 6s 8d for erecting and taking down the scaffold and 2s 8d for a quart of ale to quench his thirst.

It is worth noting that the machine is referred to as female more than a decade before a similar reference to its gender in the Edinburgh records. It was unlikely to be linked to the Iron Maiden of Nuremberg, which resembled an Egyptian mummy lined with iron spikes. There might have been some religious significance in this – an effigy called The Maiden was used in festive processions in pre-Reformation Scotland. Perhaps it was a macabre joke – a backhanded compliment to Queen Mary – or it might have been regarded as female by its makers, the craftsmen, in the same affectionate way that mariners regard ships. It has also been suggested the appellation came from the Gaelic, *Mod-dun*, which originally signified the place where justice was administered. The true meaning seems lost in history. The Maiden was last used in Aberdeen in 1615 when Francis Hay was beheaded for the murder of Adam Gordon, brother of the Laird of Gight.

There was an old belief that Mary witnessed Sir John Gordon's execution by the Maiden in the Castlegate after the Battle of Corrichie in 1562. The combatants on one side were the supporters of the Queen and those on the other were followers of Sir John's father, the proud and powerful Earl of Huntly, who dropped dead from his horse after his army was routed. A distraught queen was forced to watch Sir John's execution performed 'by a butcherlie fellow, that stroke his head off with many blowes'. While Sir John was honourably butchered by a swordsman, five of his men were hanged, a punishment beneath his station.

Even after the demise of the headsman the famous and infamous continued to have their limbs spiked after dying on the gallows. In 1636, a notorious freebooter Gilderoy, real name Patrick McGregor, and nine of his gang were captured after terrorising Deeside and Strathdon. (Gilderoy's Cave is located at the Burn o' Vat, which flows into Loch Kinord, Dinnet.) They were eventually hanged on a tall gibbet at Edinburgh Cross. Their heads and right hands were struck off and exhibited on town gates throughout Scotland. John Hector, a jailor, was paid for exhibiting the heads of the McGregor gang in Aberdeen.

The same fate awaited the royalist military leader James Graham, Marquis of Montrose. In Edinburgh, in May 1650, he was 'half-hanged' (taken down while still alive) on a lofty gibbet and then decapitated.

His head was stuck on Edinburgh's tolbooth, while the rest of his body parts were dispersed to Stirling, Perth and Aberdeen. One of his hands remained on view on a pinnacle of Aberdeen tolbooth for ten years before being returned to his family in a coffin draped with crimson velvet after the Reformation.

When powerful lairds dominated Scottish life, they had the choice of condemning criminals to the pit or the gallows – that is, serving time in a prison pit or death by hanging. During this age of 'pit and gallows', felons were also hanged from living trees. 'Dool' or 'dule' (grief or sorrow) trees grew in the grounds of several castles, including Fyvie in Aberdeenshire. A few specimens still exist in Aberdeenshire – at Leith Hall, Rhynie, Edinglassie Castle, near Huntly, and Inverey, near Braemar. The Gallows Tree o' Mar carries a terrible curse, invoked centuries ago by a heartbroken widow whose son was hanged for cattle rustling by the powerful Farquharsons of Inverey. She predicted the 'dool, dark pine' would flourish long after the Farquharsons had left Deeside. By 1805 the direct male line of the Farquharsons had withered and died. The tree slid into a sand hole eighty years ago and is now supported by cables. The 'hangman's tree' at Enzean, Monymusk, was cut down in 1947. The site of the gallows in Kirkwall, Orkney, is now a flowerbed.

A curious execution relic in Deeside was turned into a wayside bench. The hanging stone of Dess, believed to be the socket for a gibbet post, was unearthed during road works at Gallows Hillock on the A93 between Kincardine O'Neil and Aboyne. Gallow stones have also been located close to the A920 at Dufftown and at Leslie Castle, near Insch.

There are other reminders of crime and punishment. Randal's Knap, a grassy hillock near Fettercairn, is where an Irish soldier, Randal Courtney, was supposed to have been hanged for housebreaking in 1743. Gallows' Howe is a hollow in a field near Hilldowntree, where the Aberdeen suburbs meet the South Deeside Road. In 1760, salmon fisher Alexander Buck was outlawed by the Circuit Court after he failed to appear on a charge of murdering William Duncan, also a salmon fisher, by pushing him over a bridge near Hilldowntree, which owes its name to a tree that took root after being washed down the Dee in 1860.

A century before Victorian executioner William Marwood perfected the 'long drop', which resulted in the instantly fatal 'hangman's fracture' of the cervical vertebrae, a condemned man would climb a double ladder propped against the gallows beam and stand on a rung while the hangman made the necessary adjustments to the noose. He was then shoved off the ladder, usually to choke to death. Sometimes the hangman swung from the felon's legs to end his agony.

When farmer John Hutcheon, cattle thief and housebreaker, of Cranabog of Carnousie, near Turriff, was carted to the gibbet in Aberdeen on 28 June 1765, he was given time to pray and read his book of devotion before he was 'thrown off'. After hanging for sometime, his body was cut down and spirited away by surgeons.

The hangman's ladder (a rare example can be seen in St Magnus Cathedral, Kirkwall) was discarded for a horse and cart. On Friday 1 November 1776, Alexander Morison, a respected Aberdeen cartwright who had murdered his maltreated wife, Agnes Yule, with an axe, was transported to the gibbet at Gallow Hill. The spectators braved stormy weather as Morison, who had been fed on bread and water since the verdict, arrived at the gibbet with Robbie Welsh. The pair never left the cart. Morison, who stood erect in a jaunty red waistcoat and a matching nightcap that was soon to mask his agony, addressed the crowd in a 'pathetic manner'. After the rope was put around his neck, Morison wedged his feet so securely to the cart that it needed the crack of a whip to drive the horse forward, leaving him swinging in space. After his execution, Morison was hung in chains. He was the last person to be executed at Gallow Hill and to have his body exhibited in a suit of iron chains in Aberdeen. Because of the historic occasion, a contemporary report noted that it was the greatest crowd ever to have watched an execution at the spot.

In the end, Morison's body was recovered by friends and the gibbet chains were dumped in the street. The chains and the burgh stocks were stored for safekeeping in St Mary's Chapel, below the East Church of St Nicholas, but were eventually acquired by a building contractor. Human skeletons were found when foundations were dug for a powder magazine at the old execution site. Excavation work years later located a number of thick chains but these were not for binding the doomed criminals – they were lightning conductors once attached to the magazine.

Hanging in chains was common in England for centuries but, with the growing crime rate in Scotland, a new act 'for better preventing of the horrid crime of murder' was implemented at Easter 1752. The bodies of executed felons would either be gibbeted or given for anatomical research. Seven months later, a man and a woman were the first criminals under the new act to be hung in chains in Aberdeen. Wife murderer William West, a seaman, would share his fate with Christian Phren, an Aberdeenshire farm servant, who had murdered her illegitimate baby and thrown it on the fire. The poor woman was brought into Aberdeen with the remains of her charred infant in her apron. Their diet was bread and water and, under the terms of the new act, they were kept in the condemned cell to await execution, rather than mix with other prisoners. On Friday 24 November, they were brought down to the Laigh Tolbooth in order to repent before their execution at Gallow Hill. West was unmoved by the presence of the provost and ministers, while the tearful woman prayed most fervently.

They were carted to the gibbet where West denied his guilt to the last. He acknowledged he had been a great sinner and he prayed for himself and Phren. At this point, he seemed so unconcerned that he actually offered to put the rope around his neck (he was probably drunk). The *Aberdeen Journal* reported, 'The poor woman gave by her penitent behaviour, great satisfaction to all present, and West (as the sea phrase is) died hard.' After hanging for half an hour, West was taken down to be fitted with a 'neat' suit of chains. His body was hung up again. Phren's body was taken down and, soon after, carried off by the surgeons. West's bleached skeleton hung undisturbed for ten years until it was dumped in the doorway of the Methodist meeting house, in Queen Street, with a label bearing the following amusing couplet pinned to its bony chest:

> I William Wast (sic) at the point of damnation,
> Request the prayers of this congregation.

Medical students might have been responsible. But there is a traditional story that youths in Old Aberdeen would dare each other to visit the grim gibbet at night. A wager was made that one of them would not go near Gallow Hill with a bowl of hot soup. A volunteer was found and, on arrival at the gibbet, presented the steaming offering to the hanged man. When a hollow voice said, 'It's too hot!', the lad replied, 'Well blow, ye bugger!' and then hotfooted it back to a High Street pub. The ghostly voice, of course, belonged to a companion hiding near the gibbet.

17

The story was passed to me by a New Zealand correspondent whose antecedents came from Old Aberdeen. A similar tale surrounds the gibbeted body of Matthew Cocklain, who murdered an old woman at Derby on Christmas Eve in 1775.

The bodies of executed criminals were usually gibbeted close to the scene of their crimes. On 7 July 1773, the body of father of nine, Kenneth Leal, an Elgin messenger at arms, was hung in chains at Janet Innes's Cairn, the spot on the high road between Elgin and Fochabers where he robbed the mail post boy of £270. A crowd of 5000, some coming from up to ten miles away, gathered at the cairn which had been erected to the last witch burned in the parish. A graphic description of the gibbet irons in the *Elgin Courant* in January 1868 relates how a number of workmen employed by John Sellar, the millwright at Longhill, were cutting timber in Sleepieshill wood, near 'Kenny's Hillock', where the gibbet had stood, when they discovered human remains two to three feet under the surface.

> The chain was first got hold of, and on pulling it up all the hoops attached to it and encircling the body were brought to light. The complete apparatus consisted of a ring round each ankle, from which a chain of ordinary make passed up either leg and was fastened to a band of strong hoop iron round the body; from this ring or band four straps of a similar construction passed over the shoulders to the ring that encircled the neck, the neck ring in its turn being attached to the head cap, which consisted of four straps passing up either side of the head and meeting at the top, where a strong swivel-link was riveted through them to allow it to turn with the wind. The body was suspended from the gibbet by a chain rather more than two feet long and made of three-eighths of an inch round iron, the links being about three inches in diameter, in the form of a common chimney 'crook'. The bones and the whole apparatus were again buried, with the exception of the head-piece and the chain to which it was riveted; these were carried as trophies to Longhill and hung dangling on the garden paling near Mr Sellar's workshop ...'

The grim find was made in 1829, the year of the Muckle Spate, when widespread flooding in August carried off people, livestock, houses, bridges and the paling with its macabre relics. Leal was the second of three criminals gibbeted in the area in eighty years.

In the year Leal was executed, the office of 'doomster' was abolished. The 'doomster', 'deemster' or 'dempster' was the court official who formally proclaimed the sentence on the prisoner at the bar. But sometimes this was performed by the executioner. In 1453, the Aberdeen Dean of Guild paid 'the dempstar' 13s 4d for his services. On Friday 2 August 1700, the Stonehaven doomster, John Fraser, performed a curious act at the execution of John Duncan, of Auchenblae, who was sentenced to death the previous month for the theft and reset. He had stolen cattle from Kerloch Hill and driven them for sale to the annual Paddy Fair, Fordoun, and to a hill market at Kirriemuir. Although John Reid, who had stolen linen from a bleaching green at Den of Morphie, near St Cyrus, escaped the noose, Sheriff James Keith ordered him to be branded on his right shoulder blade and to be bound to the condemned man on the journey to Gallow Hill at Dunnottar. Reid was forced to watch the execution and then bury Duncan at the gallows' foot. The final insult came at the end when the doomster kicked Reid, probably on the backside, and he was banished from the shire for life. If he returned, he faced instant death.

Four months earlier, Alexander Matheson and Christian Welsh were found guilty of resetting goods that had been stolen by John Erskine, a fugitive thief whom they had harboured in their home, and were whipped through Stonehaven by the common hangman. They were fettered by the arms, in company with Erskine, and carted from the tolbooth to the gallows. After they had watched Erskine hang, the couple were kicked by the hangman and banished, never to return, under pain of death. In the nineteenth century, workmen planting trees on Gallow Hill exhumed bones belonging to people who had been hanged there.

In July 1748, the Aberdeen hangman James Chapman pronounced doom upon Alexander Cheyne, a young Fyvie man who was a member of a gang of robbers which roamed the countryside, torturing people and pillaging and burning property. The judges promised to spare him from the gallows if he named his accomplices but he refused and he was executed by Chapman in the Castlegate, Aberdeen.

After the Forty-five Uprising was crushed, there followed a wave of robberies and outrages in north-east Scotland by roaming bands of outlawed rebels. The attacks were mainly directed at manses. At the beginning of 1748, James Davidson, who had deserted the British army to support the Jacobites, was arrested after a robbery at Cortachy in Angus. He had committed several other robberies in Angus and the Mearns. At the Spring Circuit Court in Aberdeen, he was found guilty, by Lords Strichen and Drummore, of housebreaking, robbery and sorning (obtaining food and lodgings without paying) and sentenced to be executed on 1 July 1748 at the Ruthrieston Crossroads, near the Bridge of Dee.

Davidson lifted the gloom of the hanging by wearing a tartan vest and breeches, white stockings, tied with blue garters, clean shirt, white gloves and a white nightcap tied with blue ribbons. He stepped briskly into the cart, which took him from the tolbooth to the gallows overlooking the old bridge. A Catholic, he read his book of devotions all the way to the gibbet.

His escort of St George's Dragoons also wore their best dress, with orange cockades in their hats to commemorate the Battle of the Boyne. He was cut down after twenty-five minutes and hung in chains. In *The Black Kalendar of Aberdeen*, a chronological record of local trials and executions dating from the early eighteenth century, it says, 'This certainly looks more like an Irish affair altogether than an execution in Scotland.'

On the walk to the gallows the tradition for many years was for the condemned person to dress in a shroud. When Alexander Philp was hanged in Aberdeen on 24 November 1749, he added a macabre fashion note to the solemn occasion by decorating his cap and gloves with blue ribbons. Alexander Macdonald, his accomplice in murder and robbery, cheated the gallows by escaping from the prison. On 31 May 1822, two murderers broke with tradition by refusing to wear grave clothes at their execution in Aberdeen. Robert Mackintosh and William Gordon, whose escape attempt from the tolbooth a week earlier was thwarted, were each dressed in black suits. It was the town's first double execution since West and Phren in 1752. During a drunken row Gordon (45), a fishing tackle maker in Aberdeen, had stabbed his wife through the femoral artery with a sharpened poker. Mackintosh (21), a farm servant from Crathie, murdered Lizzie Anderson (40), who was pregnant by him, by slashing her throat with a razor. Mackintosh had been courting another woman and was unhappy at the prospect of being a father. He had also failed to persuade Lizzie to surrender a letter in which he promised to marry her.

The scene on the scaffold was appalling. Gordon died without a struggle but the noose had been improperly fitted around Mackintosh's neck and he gave a scream of pain when the drop fell. His body convulsed for several minutes and the huge crowd of spectators uttered their disgust. Before the execution, Mackintosh's father had made a vain journey to London to try to get remission of that part of Lord Gillies' sentence that ordered his son's body to be dissected. He failed and, to add insult to injury, Mackintosh's skeleton was exhibited in the university's anatomical museum. Gordon's body was also handed over to the surgeons.

The horror of dissection forced friends and relatives of the hanged to smuggle the corpses out of the reach of the anatomists. In March 1753, James Miller, a habitual thief, was whipped through the streets of Aberdeen days after he was caught breaking into a house in Inverurie. When sentenced to hang at the Gallow Hill on 16 November, he pleaded with the judges for a light in his cell to read the Bible. After his body was cut down, he was buried at the foot of the gallows. But some friendly seamen rescued it from the surgeon's knife by taking it to sea in a yawl and sinking it. John Barnet or McBarnet, from Kirktown of Peterhead, arrested at the end of 1817 for theft by housebreaking, broke prison with two others. His wanted notice, which offered a reward, described him as a 'stout man, of about five feet nine or ten inches in height, with brown hair and red whiskers, with a downcast and thoughtful look'. He was rearrested and executed in November 1818. His body was buried at sea but, within two or three days, it came ashore at the mouth of the River Don and fell to the anatomists.

Some found a way to avoid the hangman's noose by taking their own lives. On the eve of his execution on 24 November 1758, James Paterson, an Aberdeen huckster condemned for theft and housebreaking, hanged himself in his cell in the tolbooth. First, Paterson, an invalid, secured his crutch to the window bars with rope twisted out of bed straw. Then he made a halter from strips of his pillowcase. He was completely stiff and cold when found the next morning.

The city's only triple execution took place at the front door of the tolbooth on 23 May 1823. Thomas Donaldson (25), William Buchanan (26) and William McLeod (20) were hanged for theft and 'stouthrief', assault of persons in their own home. McLeod and his younger brother,

Neil, who were in custody for a capital offence, broke out of the jail, along with Donaldson and two others some weeks before their trials. While on the run, the McLeods forced their way into Margaret Murray's house at Rathen, near Fraserburgh, and robbed her.

Donaldson and Buchanan were accused of savagely assaulting and robbing John Cooper, a seventy-year-old farmer, of Newton of Greens, Monquhitter. Cooper walked a distance of thirty miles into Aberdeen to give evidence at their trial but, on his return home, took to his bed and died. A plea for mercy for Donaldson, Buchanan and McLeod failed and, on the afternoon of the execution, the condemned men delivered a powerful oration from the scaffold against the evils of the tap-room and gaming house. A public subscription organised by young members of the incorporated trades paid for their mourning attire. The drop fell at 3.25 p.m. They appeared not to suffer, with only a slightest convulsion from Donaldson and Buchanan. It is probable that these benefactors were the same persons who had promised to bury them with dignity. After the bodies were cut down, they were interred in a single grave at the Gallow Hill. Probably because of his age, Neil McLeod was eventually transported for life instead of being hanged.

The Banff scaffold created a legend on 16 November 1700 when they hanged Highland freebooter James Macpherson. He was second only in name to the legendary Rob Roy. After escaping the law several times, Macpherson was cornered at Keith Fair by a local laird, Duff of Braco, and his men. Macpherson put up a stiff resistance but was overpowered after a sword fight in the kirkyard.

Tradition has it that Macpherson, a talented musician, played the fiddle as he was carted to the gibbet on Gallow Hill at Banff. On the gallows platform, he offered to give the instrument to any member of his clan who would play it over his body at his lykewake (the ritual of keeping a nocturnal watch over the dead). But, when his offer was greeted with silence, he smashed the fiddle over the executioner's head and then hanged himself! Some claimed that a reprieve was on its way. When the magistrates were told that a messenger had been seen from the Gallowhills crossing the Bridge of Banff, they apparently wound forward the hands of the town clock to hurry along the execution. It was said the magistrates were stripped of their powers of trying and executing felons.

But the facts are that Macpherson did not die alone as the Banff records show – 'Payed to the executioner for tows (rope) att executione of McPherson and Gordon, £1.' The execution took place at Banff Cross between two and three in the afternoon on a market day, in accordance with the sentence of the court. The magistrates would not have risked conveying a high-risk prisoner all the way to the Gallowhill. He was accompanied to the scaffold by an equally notorious rogue, James Gordon, a member of his gang.

Macpherson would have been unable to play the fiddle if, as was customary, his hands were bound. Moreover the Bridge of Banff had not yet been built and the burgh continued to hang criminals after his death. Whatever the truth of the story, the fiddle, or what remained of it, was placed in the MacPherson's Museum in Newtonmore. And the rogue's name lives on through the words of Sir Walter Scott and Robert Burns' fine song, 'Macpherson's Lament', set to the fiddle tune, 'Macpherson's Rant'.

But hangmen also died. In 1588 an Aberdeen shoemaker, John Wishart, was murdered by the town's executioner. James Paterson got a taste of his own medicine when he was hanged and his head spiked on the Justice Port.

On dark and windy nights the rattle and eerie whine of chains ensured folk gave Alexander Gillan's gibbeted corpse on Stynie Moor a wide berth. It was whispered that his ghost haunted the bleak spot near Fochabers, Moray, where he had committed a foul murder and where he would eventually suffer at the hands of an incompetent hangman. One Sunday in August 1810, Gillan (19) set off across the moor from his employer John Thomson's farm at Stynie, with the intention of visiting relatives in the nearby village of Lhanbryde. On the way, he met ten-year-old Elspet Lamb, whose sister had rejected the hot-headed Thomson who worked as a farm servant. Elspet was herding cattle belonging to her father, John Lamb, who farmed Nether Newton. Dark juices swam within Gillan. He ravished the girl then battered her to death with a boulder. Instead of continuing his journey to Lhanbryde, he attended morning service in Speymouth parish church, better known as the Red Kirk because of its red-harled walls, where he was arrested. Bloodstained clothing and his staff, cut from a tree before he committed the murder, were found at the scene.

The following month at the Circuit Court in Inverness, Gillan was found guilty of rape and murder and sentenced to be gibbeted on Stynie Moor. The judge, Charles Hope, Lord Justice Clerk, raged at Gillan:

> I look upon any punishment you can receive in this world as mercy. Did you flatter yourself that if you escaped detection here, you could have lived or taken your place among the industrious in the peaceful occupations of men? If so, you greatly deceived yourself. The mangled corpse of this innocent would have unceasingly haunted you. Her departed spirit would have drawn aside your curtain at midnight, and horror and despair would have driven you to take vengeance upon yourself.

The eye of God never slept, the judge warned, and, by going to the church after his crime, the condemned man thought he would hide his guilt amongst the people of God. Instead, the House of God, to which he had impiously fled to cover his wickedness, became a means of bringing his guilt to light.

Gillan betrayed no emotion as the Lord Justice Clerk, passing sentence, said it was decreed that the prisoner should be deprived of a Christian burial. He would make Gillan a 'more lasting and memorable example of the fate which awaits the commission of such sins as yours'. His spine-tingling judgement continued:

> The particular situation of the country where this crime was committed, its extensive and vast woods; its uninhabited moors, and the solitude which reigns over it are but too well calculated for purposes such as yours: I am therefore anxious that these solitary woods and extensive wilds may be traversed by every person of both sexes at all times, and even on the hours of night, with confidence and security. It is my duty to make them as safe as the streets of a city. I have therefore determined that after your execution, you shall be hung in chains, until the birds of the air pick the flesh off you body, and your bones bleach and whiten in the winds of heaven, thereby to afford a constant warning of the fatal consequences which inevitably attend the indulgence of the passions; and hoping that the example may operate in the prevention of crimes; and secure the more permanent safety of the people.

Gillan spent the last few days of his life on bread and water in the quaint, three-storey tolbooth which once dominated Elgin's marketplace. On Wednesday 14 November 1810, Gillan was conveyed to Stynie Moor in a cart, with the Inverness hangman William Taylor and the gibbet irons, which had been made by Elgin blacksmiths, in another. An escort was provided by town's officers and troops of the 78th Regiment (Seaforths), stationed at Fort George. It was reported by the *Inverness Journal* that an 'immense concourse of people, from every quarter and of every age and sex', followed the official party.

Gillan who wore white mittens over his shackled hands broke down and was unable to read a piece of paper he clutched in his hand. It was rumoured to be a lurid confession but it proved to be quotations from religious tracts. But he managed to climb the ladder to the scaffold to await his fate. However, there was a delay while Taylor haggled over his 'perks' of office – namely, the prisoner's clothes. Or, as the press put it, 'He was detained in this state of awful suspense too long, by the unskilfulness of the executioner, whose concern seemed directed to the perquisites of the office more than the business in which he was engaged.'

After the drop, Gillan's dead body hung for an hour before it was taken down and put in irons. The *Inverness Journal* described the gibbeting as:

> A shocking example of the dreadful effects of vice, when permitted to usurp the empire of reason; an example which, it is hoped, will strike deep into the minds of the rising generation, and tend to prevent the recurrence of such terrifying spectacles.

The day after the execution the registrar in the nearby parish of Urquhart made the following entry in his records:

> A.G. was a good-looking young man but had always been of a stubborn, disobedient temper and licentious conversation. Till after his condemnation he seemed to have no proper sense of his crime. He then began to relent and suffered apparently very penitently. His body may be seen hanging in chains very distinctly from both sides of Urquhart. But particularly from the west side of the churchyard by standing on Elspet Lamb's grave.

It was remarkable, it was noted, that the places where three criminals had been gibbeted were within sight of each other. He was referring to Gillan, Kenneth Leal, the mail robber, and a murderer called McGregor, executed in the 1730s.

Hangman Taylor's callousness on the drop had not been forgotten and, sometime after, he received an anonymous letter informing him that a new executioner was required in Aberdeen. Taylor set out to apply for the office but, on his way through Elgin, he was set upon by a mob. He was badly maltreated and dragged to the top of Ladyhill in a cart which was then rolled down the steep slope. The hapless hangman momentarily gave his tormentors the slip and made his way to a farm where a cart was sent to carry him to Forres. He was caught again and unceremoniously dumped out of the cart into an open shed at Drumduan, where he was found dead next morning. He was buried in 'Hell's Hole' on Cluny Hill at Forres. Years later an elderly Elgin woman told a local author that the hangman was 'set upon by the soutars (shoemakers), who chased him out of the town, prodding him with their awls'. Taylor waded across the River Lossie, above the Haugh, giving the spot the name of 'Hangman's Ford'.

On 20 March 1811, the *Aberdeen Journal* reported:

> We understand a precognition is going on before the Sheriff of Elgin, regarding certain circumstances which are said to have occasioned the death of the miserable creature who acted as executioner in this place, when on his way through Elgin to Aberdeen. From his well known habits, it is highly probable that his death is more to be ascribed to the effects of drunkenness and cold than to any inhumanity on the part of the people of Elgin.

Despite the superior opinion of Elgin folk, the *Inverness Journal* reported from the Circuit Court in Inverness the following month, 'James McCurroch and John Dawson, shoemakers apprentices, from Elgin, accused of assaulting, stabbing and otherwise maltreating William Taylor, late executioner at Inverness, while at Elgin, were found guilty, and sentenced to be transported beyond seas for seven years.' The judge was Lord Hermand.

Gillan's body vanished overnight but his gallows served as a macabre landmark until 1911, when the landowner, the Duke of Richmond, agreed it was a public nuisance and it should be removed and buried on the spot. Human bones were disturbed but whether they belonged to the murderer or a suicide is unclear. A small cross of oak made, it was claimed, from his gallows, was erected.

But Taylor was not the last Scottish executioner to suffer a violent death. On 14 August 1847, the ill-fated John Scott, Aberdeen's last resident hangman, was killed by an alcoholic yards from his home in Old Fishmarket Close in Edinburgh. Scott, who had suffered the wrath of Johnny Milne's widow, was lured back to Edinburgh, where he had been assistant hangman, by higher wages – 12 shillings weekly, with £5 pounds per annum from the exchequer. He also received additional payments for each execution and flogging he performed. His new job title was 'official executioner to the City of Edinburgh and "doomster" to the High Court of Justiciary'. His regular wages and perks were paid by Edinburgh Corporation.

Scott's killer was John Edey (39), a broker and seller of watches in the Cowgate, who pleaded not guilty to a charge of culpable homicide at the capital's High Court of Justiciary on 5 November 1847. Scott had died of brain and kidney damage as a result of heavy blows to his head or neck and the body. In his defence, Edey declared he had known Scott but bore no ill-will towards him. He had abstained from alcohol for seven years until the fateful day when he went boozing with friends. He had been so drunk that he had no recollection of the crime.

James McLevy, the celebrated Edinburgh detective, gave evidence on Edey's behalf. He knew both the prisoner and the deceased and described Edey as 'quiet, honest and sober'. Evidence by McLevy that Scott had been severely assaulted by a young man called Wilson a few weeks before the fatal attack was perhaps an attempt to show that Edey had not been entirely to blame for the hangman's injuries. Scott's widow told the court that her husband had been in very delicate health for years and confirmed Wilson's assault on him. The jury found Edey guilty but urged leniency and he got nine months' imprisonment.

3

FALSE TONGUES

In 1909, American escapologist Harry Houdini, manacled and bound in chains, dived off the bridge of a tug into the cold and choppy waters of the Aberdeen navigation channel. Thousands cheered as he freed himself and returned in triumph to Pocra Quay at Footdee – or 'Fittie' as this old fishing village was, and is, known. But the history of Pocra Quay stretches back much further than that and there was a time when the inhabitants of Fittie faced an ordeal that would have tested Houdini.

For centuries Pockraw, literally 'fishing net row', was a shingly haven for small fishing boats from Footdee, a fiercely independent community but now a city suburb, at the mouth of the Dee. Strangers were treated with caution. Four hundred years ago, an outbreak of vandalism at the haven was brought to the attention of the provost and magistrates of Aberdeen. On 22 May 1600, shipmasters complained that their vessels were being cast adrift, causing them 'gryt hurt and henderance'. It seems the mooring ropes of boats owned by strangers and some locals were deliberately cut or tossed into the water by fishers seeking a more favourable berth.

The town council acted with great severity and warned that 'ony inhabitant of the said toune of Futtie, man or woman', convicted of these offences would be tied to a stake within the flood mark for three hours, while the water swirled around the malefactor. Afterwards the half-drowned culprit was to be scourged through the streets and banished for life from Aberdeen and Footdee. The cruel punishment reflected life in bygone times when justice was swift and brutal. In the previous century, the country was gripped by lawlessness with offenders being punished for crimes which ranged from hamesucken (assaulting a person in their home) to murder.

In the mid-sixteenth century, the Reformation saw the rise of the all-powerful Kirk. Through its general assembly and church sessions, it unleashed, a bizarre range of humiliating punishments on parishioners who broke its strict moral code, which covered adultery, fornication, drunkenness and not going to church on a Sunday. The jougs, which consisted of a hinged collar and a padlock to secure the neck of the wrongdoer, was a common instrument of ecclesiastical punishment in Scotland from the sixteenth century onwards. It was attached by a chain to the wall of the parish church or the gallows, whipping post or market cross. At the old cross in Fettercairn market square, attached to the cross, you can see an iron hasp and this is all that remains of the town's jougs.

On 15 April 1595, Aberdeen magistrates ordered Alexander Ewan, the Dean of Guild, to arrange for a pair of jougs to be fixed to the gibbet, at the cost of £1, for punishing 'commoun flyteris (foul-mouthed) and sklanderous persones'. Four years later Marjorie Hacket was put in the jougs for slander. In 1707 William Smith was paid 14s for making a 'pair of jeugs' for use in Old Aberdeen.

The Kirk set a strict dress code for congregations, resulting in more subdued fashions. The wives of Aberdeen burgesses were expected to wear decent cloaks, but never plaids, and to hear sermons in full view of the preacher. Only harlots were allowed to wear plaids covering their head at church or market. Maids who dressed in ruffs or red hoods risked having the offending items ripped off and trampled in the gutter.

There were other forms of humiliation. In May 1759, three Aberdeen women, Janet Shinnie, Margaret Barrack and Mary Duncan were convicted of receiving goods stolen from a local merchant. They were tied to a stake at the market cross by the common hangman, with nooses about their necks and papers denoting their crimes pinned to their breasts. Their ordeal lasted twenty-four hours. It ended with them being driven off in a cart and banished from the burgh. To add to their shame, their heads were shaved and they were dogged by the hangman, the town drummer and a jeering crowd. Edward Raban, the 'Laird of Letters', who had a workshop near the cross in the previous century, was contracted by the town council to print papers which were 'prined on the bristis' of culprits pilloried at the scaffold.

Rogues were drummed out of Banff and ritually kicked on to the ferry boat which plied across the River Deveron. Felons were pilloried and made to bear notices such as 'Infamous Notorious Thief' or 'A Receptor of Stolen Goods'.

In March 1792, a servant at the Mill of Boyndlie stood bound and bareheaded at Banff Cross, bearing label saying, 'Alexander Scott, an Infamous Swindler and Cheat.' He was drawn through the streets of the burgh in a cart while the town drummer beat the 'Rogue's March'. His humiliation continued in nearby Portsoy before he was banished from Banffshire.

In 1764, a father and son were drummed out of Cullen for 'debauching the morals' of the townsfolk. James Peterkin and his son Arthur were guilty of running schoolboys into debt through card-playing and selling them gingerbread. To settle their debts, the boys resorted to theft. The Peterkins were jailed and, after their release, carried, with their hands tied behind their backs, from one end of the burgh to the other, with the town drummer marching behind. The labels on their chests bore the message in large letters, 'A Receipter of Stolen Goods and Corrupter of Youth'. They were banished for-ever from the town and warned, should they return, they would be whipped and imprisoned.

Persons who fell into debt were physically punished and further humiliated by wearing the 'dyvours' habit' – a coat of yellow and brown halves and stockings, cape or hood in the same colours. Before he was released from custody, John Crichton wore the habit when led from Banff tolbooth to stand for an hour at the cross on market day. The practice was abolished during the reign of William IV (1830–37).

In 1810, Elspet Hoyes, alias Anstie, of Forres, jailed at Inverness for a year for housebreaking, stood in public at Elgin bearing a label inscribed, 'A Notorious Thief'.

Insulting your neighbour usually landed the offender in trouble. During the Aberdeen witch panics in the sixteenth and seventeenth centuries, few were safe from malicious gossip, whatever their station in life. Marjorie Mearns was forced to beg forgiveness in church for slandering a widow by calling her a witch. Her punishment was to grovel on her knees before the widow and congregation and utter the words, 'False tongue, ye lied!'

In 1643, in presence of witnesses, William Cook spat out, 'Dirt in your teeth, vain fellow!', at Andrew Meldrum, a dyer. He was locked up in jail until he paid a fine of £4 to the Dean of Guild and apologised in front of the magistrates.

In 1582, William Ronaldson, a cloth-maker, was summoned to the Aberdeen town house in the Castlegate where, as punishment for slandering weaver David Castle, he got down on his knees before the provost and magistrates and the offended party to beg their forgiveness. To refuse would have meant banishment.

The branks, or scold's bridle, was an ecclesiastical punishment reserved for women offenders – nagging wives, gossips, scaremongers, suspected witches and fornicators. It was an iron frame that enclosed the head in a close-fitting cage. An iron gag prevented speech and the hapless victim was led by a chain attached to the bridle. There are two grotesque examples in Montrose Museum. One bears a spike representing a tongue while the other is an iron mask. The Dunnottar parish church branks is in Marischal Museum, Aberdeen.

In Old Aberdeen in 1701, Marjorie Garioch was fined and 'brankit' for bad-mouthing weaver James Fraser and his wife by calling him a 'land-lowper' (vagabond) and 'beggar fellow' and accusing her of escaping banishment seven years previously.

But sometimes men were 'brankit', usually for sexual offences. In 1591, Patrick Pratt was locked in the branks at the market cross in Aberdeen for committing the 'horrible and heinous crime' of incest. On his head he wore a paper crown advertising his crime. He was also forced to stand barefoot and barelegged in a hair shirt at the Kirk door, followed by a spell at the 'pillar' or high stool of repentance that stood near the pulpit.

The less conspicuous laigh (low) stool was for those whose offences were less serious in the eyes of church courts. In Aberdeen in 1603, Janet Knowles, unable to pay a fine for fornication (she was either unwed or had committed adultery), had her head shaved and was placed in the jougs. She then stood in the stool of repentance in church the following Sunday. Isobel Coutts, of Aberdeen, also suffered when she was accused of fornication and prostitution. She sat on the church stool for three Sundays before she was imprisoned in the vault of St Nicholas Church, where she was fed bread and water. Her head was shorn and she was put in the jougs at the Mercat Cross. Janet Will, servant, convicted of adultery with her master at Strichen, sat in the stool for six months. But because she did not appear sufficiently repentant she was locked in the jougs.

Swearing in public fetched a fine of 12d in Aberdeen and the penniless were placed in the cuckstool or 'goffis' and forced to wear a paper crown. Habitual swearing at the table resulted in similar punishment while a third conviction for the same offence meant instant banishment. In England, the cuckstool was originally a commode used for punishing nagging women. In Scotland, the term was applied to the stocks and the pillory, two different implements of punishment but with the same purpose. The cuckstool, which was first mentioned in the Domesday Book as punishment reserved for brewers of bad ale, was a degrading method of chastisement in Aberdeen from 1405, when it was ruled:

> Whosoever shall abuse the town baillies, or any of the king's officers, shall kiss the cuckstool for the first offence and be fouled with eggs, dung, mud and suchlike for the second offence, and for the third offence they shall be banished from the town for a year and a day.

Records of banishments were kept in case the culprit returned to the burgh before the time limit had expired. The punishment meant the burgh would no longer be responsible for the banished person's upkeep although he or she would, no doubt, just become a burden on some other place.

After a woman was placed in the cuckstool at Cullen in 1721, she was drummed out of town. By 1730, the Cullen cuckstool was in a state of disrepair but, after repairs, it was deemed safe enough for a culprit to stand in it for two hours. A placard bearing details of his crime – he had cut down an ash tree – was displayed on a board. His punishment included a £50 fine and imprisonment. He also had to find caution, a sum of money deposited as security for future good conduct – in his case, this meant keeping the peace for two years.

The Aberdeen magistrates probably regretted inflicting the pillory on a well-known character after they had convicted her of reset and keeping a bawdy house. Margaret Sim, who was better known as 'Lucky Walker', lived with her husband, John Walker, in Guardhouse

Close. After she was locked up for two weeks in the tolbooth, she was drummed out of town on Friday 14 April 1786. But first she was forced by the hangman to stand bareheaded on the pillory at the tolbooth stairhead, with a label proclaiming, 'Infamous Bawd and Receipt of Theft', pinned to her breast. During the hour she was there she raged and insulted the magistrates and three clergymen, Abercrombie, Hogg and Shaw, who were responsible for her plight. Her parting shot, aimed at the magistrates, no doubt caused laughter and some consternation:

> It's ill on their pairt to use me this way – for there is nae een o them that has nae been well entertained in my hoose, wi' a' thing that they wantit; except Provost Cruden – and I will except him!

The wife of a Chelsea pensioner, Jean Watt, who had stolen the duffel cloak she sold to 'Lucky', was also banished.

The stocks, a punishment more associated with Merrie England, were once a familiar sight in Scottish marketplaces. In 1685, Alexander Christal was paid 14s for mending and providing a lock for the stocks at Old Aberdeen. The stocks consisted of a bench and two wooden beams, with hinges at one end to lift the upper beam and hasps and staples at the other for padlocks to trap the culprit's feet in apertures. Only a few examples exist in Scotland. The Fraserburgh stocks were in the custody of the local burgh surveyor until they became ruinous at the beginning of the twentieth century. A replica set is displayed at Fraserburgh Heritage Centre. A replica of the Inverbervie stocks is in Stonehaven Tolbooth Museum. The Courtbook of the Barony of Leys at Crathes notes the case of James Paterson who unlawfully retrieved his horse which had been impounded by a court officer in May 1623. Paterson was put in the Banchory stocks for twenty-four hours, ordered to pay the laird, Sir Thomas Burnett of Leys, the sum of £40 and had his goods and gear confiscated.

The ducking stool was another beloved spectator sport. It consisted of a long timber beam, evenly balanced on a pivot, with a small chair at one end. The culprit was strapped in the chair while the operator, usually the hangman, took up his position at the other end and would proceed to 'duck' the wretched victim in a loch, river or harbour.

In Aberdeen 'ducking at the cran (crane)' was reserved for fornicators, blasphemers and petty criminals. Women singled out by the Kirk as being immoral were the chief sufferers. The crane was used for lifting heavy goods at the Quayhead. In November 1602, Janet Shearer, who had been exiled from Aberdeen for harlotry, made the mistake of returning. She was imprisoned in the kirk vault and ordered to be ducked and thereafter banished. However, on paying a fine of ten merks (one merk = 13s 4d Scots) she was spared the punishment.

One poor woman suffered the indignity of being ducked and whipped once a week in Aberdeen from July 1638 to May 1639! The *Aberdeen Observer* of 4 October 1833 recalled the shocking case of the frail female who, on the orders of the Kirk Session, was 'cartit from the mercat croce to the Kay-heid, thair to be dowked, at the cran, and to be quhipped everie Monday during that space.' Whatever her crime, the punishment was unusually vicious.

The searing bite of the lash was inflicted on culprits, whatever their age or sex. The 'cat o nine tails', birch rod or forked strap, which churchmen used on recalcitrant parishioners during the Reformation, were wielded with relish. Old Aberdeen, in line with other Scottish towns, employed its own scourger, who usually doubled as hangman. In 1636, Archibald Bishop, who was authorised to round up beggars and vagabonds, had the authority to deputise two persons to help subdue an unruly culprit. Refusal to help or any attempt to free the beggar could lead to the wrong-doer losing three weeks' wages, serving a spell in the local tolbooth or having to pay a fine.

For stealing a shirt in Old Aberdeen in April 1608, Isobel Jamieson, of Foveran, Aberdeenshire, was tied to the market cross and 'tirrit' (stripped) from her waist up and flogged. The punishment continued as she was marched through the streets and banished from the bishopric 'never to return under the pain of death'.

On 22 September 1652, the hangman James Anderson scourged a notorious thief, Margaret Strachan, on the stretch of high road between the Kirk and the Spitalhill, the burgh boundary with Aberdeen, where the woman was warned that, if she ever set foot in the town again, she would be drowned 'without doome or law'.

In June 1640, Margaret Warrack was detained in the Aberdeen Correction House until she confessed the 'sin of fornication' with

James Aberdeen and, to loosen her tongue, the Kirk Session ordered her to be whipped at the stake.

In October 1662, William Brutchie was appointed the official scourger in Aberdeen at a wage of 13s 4d a week. He was also given free accommodation in a dwelling house which had been specially converted from 'tuo little houses under the Gallowgate Port'. Brutchie might have also held the post of burgh hangman.

In eighteenth-century Aberdeen, whipping was carried out at three stations: the tolbooth stairhead; the head of St John's Wynd; and the Bow Brig, which spanned the Denburn and marked the western limits of the burgh. Military floggings were particularly nasty. Joshua Smith, a private whose regiment was garrisoned in Aberdeen, in 1752, received 800 lashes for theft.

In 1772, Adam Frain, a barber's apprentice, was flogged by the 'hangie' at the stairhead and the Bow Brig, jailed and banished from the county for life. He had been convicted of breaking into Aberdeen advocate John Durno's house and stealing books and banknotes. The sheriff warned him, if he returned to the county, he would be 'apprehended, incarcerated, whipt and again banished'. Adam Frain was thirteen years old!

The flogging stations in Keith, Banffshire, in the eighteenth century were located at the front of the town house and at three places in the main square while, in Banff, they were at the market cross, kirk stile, the foot of the Water Path, the Grey Stone and at the head and foot of the Back Path. After cattle thief Alexander Stuart was released from Banff tolbooth and banished on 15 July 1748, he was warned that, if he returned, he would be given six lashes by the hangman at each of these places. Stuart had earlier stood at the market cross with a placard bearing the message in large letters, 'An Infamous Outhounder of Thieves', which suggested that he instigated thefts.

In Banff in 1629, thief Isobel Mitchell was 'ordanit to be presentlie strippet nakit and scurgit out of this burgh and perpetuallie banischit'. When Duncan Macdonald took up his duties as executioner at Banff in 1693, his first duty was to flog two culprits – one was his predecessor, a man named Allister, and the other was a Donald Ross – for a fee of 12s. Their offences are not recorded.

Strangers who begged around Cullen and Deskford in 1614 were chased away by William Mackie, the official scourger.

Public floggings did not always go to plan. On Friday 13 June 1766, two soldiers and a civilian, who were found guilty at the Circuit Court in Aberdeen of carrying off meal from a ship during a riot at Banff, were sentenced to be whipped through Aberdeen and banished to the plantations for life. Walter Annesley and John Blair, of the Sixth Regiment of Foot, and Alexander Robb, of Banff, were taken from the tolbooth under military guard to be whipped by the hangman. But an angry mob intervened and attacked the 'hangie' and the guard with clubs and a hail of stones. The culprits were spirited away and, despite the Riot Act being read, the disturbance continued. The magistrates offered a reward of twenty guineas (£21) for information leading to the arrest of one or more of the escapees and an additional ten guineas for the arrest of the ringleaders. But the rescued and their rescuers had vanished.

Branding and mutilation, such as boring holes in tongues, cutting off ears or nailing ears to the pillory, were regarded as common punishments. A red-hot door key or a fiery branding iron, bearing the letter 'T' for thief, would be applied to the cheek, shoulder blade, hand or arm. The mark of a criminal proved counterproductive for it made it difficult for the victim to find honest employment which, in turn, led to them in all probability continuing their criminal ways.

In August 1699, a young boy, Patrick Falconer, who was known to be a habitual thief, was found guilty of stealing from church property in Old Aberdeen. He was punished by having his 'lugg' nailed to a stake, being burned on the cheek and then being banished from the town. In 1531, twenty-two persons were banished from neighbouring Aberdeen for a year and a day for their immoral behaviour. 'Lady' Low, who ran a brothel in the Green, was ordered to lock up and leave with all her household. The magistrates cautioned her to be on her good behaviour for seven years or be branded on the cheek but Low returned within the year. She was burned on the underside of the hand before being sent packing with the additional threat of being drowned in a sack if she came back. Undaunted, Low again showed face. She was not drowned. Instead, the hangman branded her on both cheeks and placed a paper crown on her head. In the presence of two magistrates, she was banished from Aberdeen for seven years and a day and no more was heard of 'Lady' Low.

In August 1577, three prostitutes, Bessie and Margaret Stevenson and one Skinner, alias Menzies, were convicted by Aberdeen magistrates of the 'fylthie cryme of fornication' with John Weir and banished from the 'gud toune', with the added threat that they would be branded if they returned.

When Gilbert Kemp, an Aberdeen butcher who had been banished for drunkenness and other petty crimes, defied the order in February 1608, he was taken to the Market Cross and threatened with a red-hot iron 'to terrifie him'. He was warned that, if he returned, he would be burned on the cheek and scourged through the town.

A Cullen woman, Isabel Paterson, volunteered to go into exile after stealing farmer John Duff's corn in 1636. If she returned, she was 'content to be taken and brunt (sic) with ane key upon the cheeke, and to be banest yis paroche yrefter'. In 1723, Helen Barclay, a 'vagabond', and her daughter, who were described as unlawful persons, agreed to be banished from the parish. If either of them returned, they would be burned on the cheek with 'ane key', flogged and banished a second time. Anyone who gave them shelter in the parish would be fined £10. But Cullen magistrates were not always so lenient. In 1696, Christian Gallant, a tailor's servant, stole from her master and was publicly scourged by the hangman, burned on the cheek and banished. Persons harbouring her faced a heavier fine of £50.

Lawbreakers branded in Stonehaven underwent the ordeal at a blacksmith's shop opposite the courthouse. After getting his ears bored with a red-hot iron, a culprit roared out 'while capering with pain', 'I would be right now if I had pendices (earrings)!'

'Riding the Stang' was a curious and humiliating custom carried out throughout Britain although, in the south of England, it was called 'Skimmington Riding'. The guilty party, usually a man who had ill-treated or cheated on his spouse, was forced to mount a timber beam that was then carried shoulder-high through the community. He was followed by a noisy procession of men, women and children banging and beating kettles, pots and pans and blowing whistles, horns and trumpets. Stops were made to proclaim the culprit's offence.

In Huntly, Aberdeenshire, in January 1734, John Fraser complained to the Duke of Gordon's representative that his neighbours had threatened him with 'riding the stang'.

Neighbours revealed that Fraser's wife, Anne Johnston, had been ill-treated by her husband. Anne and ten other women petitioned the duke to grant them 'toleration of the stang'. Fraser was given twenty-four hours to keep his word that he would be a good husband. But, next day, he was seized by four men and forced to ride a wind-blown tree through Huntly. Fraser complained to the laird and his tormentors were fined £20 and told to pay him £12 in compensation. The Courtbook of Banff records two cases. On 26 January 1747, Alexander Clark, journeyman shoemaker, and several others were fined £3 for causing Walter Ellis, wheelwright, and James Cooper, blacksmith, to 'ride the stang'. The hapless victims were hurt and bruised by the experience, described as 'contrair to all law and against the rules of a well-governed burgh'.

A military version of 'riding the stang' was used to punish drunken infantrymen. The 'Timmer Mare', also known as the 'German Mare', was introduced into Scottish garrison towns in Cromwellian times when victims were forced to ride the horse with a drinking cup balanced on their heads. The life-size wooden horse had a sharp-ridged back, which ensured the rider suffered an agonising induction to equestrianism. To add to their discomfort the victims' hands were tied behind their backs and muskets strapped to their feet.

During the Scottish Civil War in 1640, a 'timmer mare' was brought to Aberdeen by General Munro's Covenanting troops and placed at the door of the guardhouse in the Castlegate. A Roundhead captain punished one of his soldiers for the sin of incontinence by ordering him to 'ryde the Meare'.

But not only soldiers suffered. The Aberdeen historian John Spalding, who has left an eyewitness account of 'The Troubles' – the wars between the Royalists and the Covenanters – recounts how a tactless remark by a seventy-two-year-old citizen resulted in a painful riding lesson. 'Daylie deboshing, drinking, night-walking, combating and sweiring' by the occupying troops did not make for good public relations and, on being told that one of Munro's men had been accidentally drowned, the foolish old man wished 'that all the rest should go the same gate (road)'.

He was jailed and then made to ride the mare or, in the words of the chronicler, 'syne rode the mare to his great hurt and pain. Thus none durst do nor speak any thing against them! Uncouth to see such discipline in Aberdeen, and painful for the trespasser to suffer!'

One night, a fierce gale destroyed the guardhouse. It is to be hoped that it also blew the accursed timber mare into the harbour.

4

TALK OF THE DEVIL

High within the clock tower of Aberdeen's Flemish-style Town House, the charter room contains a set of curious documents. They make blood-chilling reading. The records, diligently kept by William Dun, Dean of Guild, in the late sixteenth century, list the expense of executing witches in the royal burgh during a horrific period of bloodlust.

The cost of loads of coal, peat and timber and other items, such as tar barrels and the stake, plus dressing and erecting it, was carefully noted in thick, black ink. Food and drink and making the iron shackles and padlocks for securing the hapless prisoners were included, along with the hangman's fee. In one day, John Justice was paid £1 6s 8d for executing four witches.

The Dean of Guild was richly rewarded by the town council with £47 3s 4d for his 'extraordinary-taking pains' in organising the execution of four pirates on the gibbet at Footdee, and at least twenty-four women and two men, one the son of a witch, strangled and then burned at Heading Hill in 1596–97, the year of the notorious witch persecutions, in Aberdeen and the north-east. Dun had also supervised repairs of the Greyfriars church steeple and the building of a stone gateway at the Bridge of Dee. The money came from the guild wine fund. The town's common servant (the hangman) received forty merks for 'awaiting on the witches' and Thomas Mollison, town clerk, got £40 for his 'pain and labours'.

The reek of human flesh and combustible substances darkened the skies over Aberdeen during the witch-hunts and the suffering of the innocent wretches who died in the name of superstition and ignorance beggars belief. King James VI of Scotland had a deep-rooted fear of witchcraft. His best-selling tract of 1597, *Daemonologie*, a commentary on the Biblical text, 'Thou shalt not suffer a witch to live', was a virtual guide on how to find, torture and convict witches. Its publication, coupled with an outbreak of plague, sparked a countrywide panic. But it was his mother, Mary, Queen of Scots, who was on the throne when an act passed by the Protestant parliament on 4 June 1563, made witchcraft legally punishable by death.

In 1590, King James personally examined the North Berwick witches at their trial at Holyrood in Edinburgh. The warlock, Dr Fian, alias John Cunningham, a schoolmaster from Prestonpans, was hideously tortured before he was burned. Dr Fian's coven was accused of raising a storm in an attempt to wreck the ship carrying the monarch and his new bride, Anne, Princess of Denmark, home to Scotland. The Aberdeen ship, *St Nicholas*, captained by John Collinson, a future provost, was one of the escorting ships. James was popular with Aberdonians, presenting the town with charters and visiting it on occasions.

Aberdeen's first witch-burning took place in 1590, when Barbara Card was 'burnt on hedownis hill'. A witch was executed a few years later for the burgh accounts carry the item, 'For the barrellis, fyre, petties, and towis, witht ane staik, to execute and burne the witche that wes burnt, £3 10s.'

The Kirk and the State played a leading part in the prosecution of persons accused of witchcraft by members of the public. Investigators relied on gossips or perhaps a neighbour with a grudge before questioning the accused, who would be incarcerated in a church vault or steeple. Torture helped loosen tongues. If sleep deprivation failed, there was always the thumbikins (thumbscrews), red-hot needles to thrust under nails or the bone-crushing 'boots'. Ruthless 'prickers' or 'jobbers' were hired to find the 'Devil's mark' on the accused's body so pity a poor suspect with a wart, mole or similar blemish. The victim was stripped, shaved and then inspected from head to toe. A brass pin was forced into the offending spot and, if the victim felt no pain or did not bleed, the test was proved.

In England, suspected witches were ducked in the nearest duck pond or river. Before 'swimming' the accused was stripped naked and tied cross-bound – her right thumb was tied to the left big toe and the left thumb tied to the right big toe. To sink meant the victim was innocent and if she remained afloat she was guilty. There is only one example of 'ducking' in Scotland and that occurred at St Andrews in 1597. A rocky pool in the River Carron, near Dunnottar Church, Stonehaven, is known as the 'Witches' Kettle'. 'Guan's Pot' in the Isla is where Keith witches were supposed to have been tested.

'The Order Pot', the name is believed to be a corruption of 'Ordeal', was a deep, dark and reed-fringed pool east of the ruined Elgin cathedral. The grim spot gave rise to a prophecy linking the Pot, the River Lossie and the cathedral:

> The Order Pot and the Lossie gray
> Shall sweep the Chan'ry Kirk away.

'The Pottie' was where criminals were drowned in Aberdeen but, despite the nearby 'Witch Hillock', an unhallowed place that was traditionally never covered by the tide, there is no recorded evidence of 'swimming' witches. There are many other places around Scotland that are named as, and claimed to have been used for, ducking witches. But these stories are only legend.

The physical and mental torture suffered by accused witches continued until the inquisitors got a full confession, preferably one involving a demonic pact between the accused and the Devil. On renouncing Christianity, a witch was given an alias. A witch burned at Slains, near Cruden Bay, was nicknamed 'Hellie Pennie'. Isobel Strachan, who bewitched the mill at Caskieben, near Inverurie, was called 'Scudder'. An Elgin witch was known as 'Bonnie Batsy'.

A royal commission of justiciary, paid for by the council, was appointed in February 1596 to try the witches at Aberdeen and, in the coming months, the king's agents went about their task with sickening gusto and soon the 'dittays'(charges), however incredulous, were mounting against alleged witches in Aberdeen, Buchan, Deeside and Banffshire. The trials were held in the courthouse library in the Aberdeen tolbooth. We know this because an item in the Dean of Guild accounts reads, 'For peittis and coilles to try thame in the librarie tua dayes befoir the execution – 6s 8d'. What was the purpose of the peat and coals? To kindle the library fire to keep the jury, which comprised of the provost, baillies, local lairds, ministers and so on, warm? Or to heat John Justice's branding irons?

The belief in witches, warlocks and demons had been widespread in Scotland, particularly in rural communities, since pagan times, when people worshipped the gods of nature. Even though the Reformed Kirk remained the cornerstone of life in the sixteenth century, the poor people still sought solace in magic and in the spirits of forests, rivers and holy wells. Until the middle of the nineteenth century, farmers still believed in the tradition of Goodman's Croft, the practice of leaving untilled and rough land as a peace offering to the Devil. The De'il's Faulie, Clooties' Croft or Halie Man's Rigs were some of the other names given to this bit of scrubland.

The witch cult survived early Christianity and, in times of sickness, the people turned to its practitioners to ease their suffering. They cured sick children, healed cattle or ensured a good harvest on land and at sea. Some witches traded in winds, to guide fishermen safely home to port or to winnow corn. Written charms were said to cure toothache. But persecutors claimed witches worked 'weel as well as woe' and the Aberdeen trials provided plenty of evidence to support these weird and wicked accusations. The Aberdeen witches met in the heart of the burgh in the dead of night. At Hallowe'en 1595, Thomas Leys, whose mother, Janet Wishart, was a prominent member of the group, led the devilish dances around the market and fish crosses in the Castlegate and the meal market. Katherine Mitchell, who testified against Thomas at the trials, said she had been knocked down by him because she had not stepped lively enough. The group was also accused of shape-changing and celebrating there in the form of hares and cats on St Katherine's Hill, now present-day Adelphi. They jigged to a Jew's harp, an instrument that was demonstrated to a delighted King James at the trial of the North Berwick witches. Janet Wishart faced thirty-one charges of witchcraft, ranging from murder – it was claimed she had bewitched two scholars into drowning themselves at Aberdeen beach – to dismembering bodies of criminals hanged at the gibbet at the Links. It made no difference that some of the alleged incidents had occurred twenty-five years earlier and that some of the witnesses were long dead. Her neighbours rounded on her.

Stabler John Pyet lay dying in his house in the Justice Port apparently because he refused to allow Janet to get her hands on his piece of land. The records described how the fevered Pyet lay in bed for eighteen weeks, melting away like a white candle and burning as if in a fiery oven. James Low, another stabler, died of the same malady after he refused to loan her his kiln and barn. Janet and Thomas were both convicted and burned at the stake and her husband, John Leys, and their daughters, Elspet, Janet and Violet, were banished from the burgh.

The Deeside witches chose a less public place for their orgies than the Aberdeen coven – the forbidding Hill of Craiglash, a broomstick's ride from Torphins and Kincardine O' Neil. There, at the Warlock Stone, on the northern slope of the hill, the group kept appointments with Auld Nick. In the sixteenth century, the 'gryt stane o' Craigleauche' stood in an open space but today it is dwarfed by forestry. The stone is damaged, broken in two. It may have been the work of superstitious farm folk or the Kirk, fearing a resurgence of the witch cult. Beatrice Robbie, who attended a meeting at Hallowe'en with her mother and sister, was indicted as a notorious witch. She was said to have come 'under the conduct of the Devil, with certain others, her devilish adherents, to Craiglash and there dancing altogether about a great stone, a long space (pace), with the Devil, her master, playing before her'. Beatrice was banished from Aberdeenshire but her mother, Margaret Ogg, was executed. Another Deeside witch, Helen Rogie, was accused of murdering her enemies by roasting their wax images in a fire. Rogie evaded capture for three days on the Hill of Learney but, when arrested, she had in her possession a 'pictour' – a lead image of a man used as a mould.

Witches suffered horribly at the stake. They were 'wirreit' (strangled) and burned but there were cases where witches were burned 'quick', that is, alive. In 1597, the following sentence was pronounced by Hutcheon, the Aberdeen doomster, on four Deeside witches, including Ogg, – 'You will be taken out betwixt the hills at afternoon, bound to a stake, and wirreit until you be deid and thereafter burnt to ashes.'

Executions in Aberdeen attracted a large proportion of the burgh's population of 7500. On the appointed day, the condemned were tied to the back of a cart and dragged to the execution site between the Castle Hill and Heading Hill. Margaret Clerk or Bain, a Lumphanan witch who was taught the black art by her sister, who had already been executed for witchcraft in Edinburgh, drew a huge crowd when she was executed in Aberdeen on 25 March 1597. Bain was the mother of the aforementioned Helen Rogie. Wooden crush barriers were smashed and town officer Thomas Dickson's halberd axe was also broken in the crush. He received £1 10s compensation to replace it. Here, for example, are the accounts relating to Margaret Bain's execution:

For sixteen loads of peats:	£1 15s
For four loads of fir:	16s
For one oil barrel:	10s
For one tar barrel:	6s 8d
For two iron barrels:	6s 8d
For three fathom of rope:	3s
For a stake, carrying and dressing it:	13s 4d
For carrying the peats, coals and barrels to the hill:	8s
For carrying of four spars to withstand the press of the people (two spars broken):	8s 8d
For John Justice for his fee:	6s 8d

The charred remains of the victims were reduced to ashes in the iron barrels, which had been heated in the fire. A fathom was a measure of length. The coal used for the burnings was stored in St Ninian's Chapel at Castle Hill.

The total expense of lodging the witches in captivity in the vault of St Nicholas Kirk, and their subsequent executions, amounted to £177 17s 4d. On one day John Justice received 13s 4d for dispatching two witches, Janet Douglas and Agnes Smellie, and an additional 6s 8d for burying two thieves at the gallows' foot. At least two Aberdeen witches cheated the hangman. The accounts note that Suppack, the alias of Helen Mackenzie, died in prison and it cost 6s 8d to bury her. Isobel Menteith hanged herself and her corpse was dragged through the streets at the tail of a cart. The cost of hiring the cart and 'earding' (burying) her was ten shillings.

The persecution of witches in Aberdeen and elsewhere continued into the next century. In 1626, Walter Baird confessed to the crime of having a conversation with the Devil and, four years later, Marion Hendry appeared before the Bishop of Aberdeen on witchcraft charges. Aberdeen's Dean of Guild's accounts for 1626–27 itemise the hire of a barrow 'to carry the crippell witches, 6s'. Andrew Clark earned £6 13s 4d for 'his paynes' in writing out charges against the witches and for acting as clerk at the court hearings. Alex Ramsay received £142 3s 4d for the upkeep of the doomed witches in the tolbooth. In November 1662, Elgin women Barbara Innes and Mary Collie, who were accused of the horrid crimes of witchcraft and renouncing their baptism to the Devil in the Moray town's Friar's Wynd, were led out of the west port to the execution site, where they were strangled and then burned. In 1631, John Philip was executed at Banff on witchcraft charges.

The last witch to be burned in Montrose was Meggie Cowie, in 1670. Meggie was blamed for raising a terrible storm which destroyed the Dronner's Dyke, built to drain a vast tract of land on the estate of Dun. In Forfar, a diorama in the Meffan Museum depicts the burning of Helen Guthrie, who implicated many innocent towns-folk in accusations of witchcraft in 1661. Helen's effigy wears the scold's bridle, which was inflicted on the Forfar witches during their imprisonment.

The major witch panics in Scotland raged during the years 1590–92, 1597, 1628–30, 1649 and 1661–62. At least 4000 were accused of witchcraft in the country but the number of those executed is likely to be lower, as not all were found guilty. But the fear of witches lingered on. Incredibly the black art was said to have been behind the tragic death of the minister of Newhills parish church, near Bucksburn, in the summer of 1715. The Rev. Robert Burnett, who was about sixty, hanged himself within the church with the bell rope. It was said the pulpit Bible was found lying open beside his body and that certain verses of the seventh chapter of Job were marked by his own hand – 'Thou scarest me with dreams and terrifiest me through visions; so that my soul chooseth strangling and death rather than my life'. It was whispered he had been the victim of witchcraft but the motive was probably suicide, following an internal dispute over his stipend.

The last witch burning in Scotland took place in 1722. Janet Horne, an eccentric old woman from Crathie, near Balmoral, was executed at Dornoch. At the execution site she warmed her hands at a blazing tar barrel and pronounced it a 'bonnie fire'.

The civic records of Aberdeen are the most complete in Scotland, with the earliest charter to be found granted by King William the Lion around 1179. The charter room contains the original Dean of Guild's accounts but, apart from a few worm-eaten pages, there is no trace of the original witchcraft trial records. Handwritten markings and notes in the margins of the fragile pages indicated they were the actual copies used in court. The records were lost for years but, in Victorian times, they were discovered among papers belonging to the town of Aberdeen. A local historical society, The Spalding Club, which took its name from Aberdeen's first historian John Spalding, borrowed the records for transcription and eventual inclusion in volume one of the *Miscellany of the Spalding Club* (1841), edited by a city advocate, John Stuart. No mention of the trial records was made in an inventory of council files ten years later. Perhaps these priceless documents, a reminder of a terrible, but important, part of the city's history, might yet turn up.

Many Scottish burgh papers relating to witchcraft have been lost in peace and war. It is a pity we cannot examine a parish record from Marykirk which read, 'Nae sermon here this day – the minister bein' awa' at Fettercairn burnin' a witch!' It raises a rare smile in a dark chapter.

It was not only the witch who was devoured by fire. Those who committed unnatural acts were also sent to the stake. At the Spring Circuit in Aberdeen in 1751, Lords Strichen and Drummore found Alexander Geddes from Kinnermony, Banffshire, guilty after trial for 'reiterated acts over eighteen years of the abominable and horrid crime of bestiality with a mare'. At five o'clock on Friday morning, 21 June 1751, he was executed in the cleft between Castle Hill and Heading Hill. After he was half-strangled, he was cut down alive and burned to ashes. According to the *Aberdeen Journal* he confessed his guilt and acknowledged the justice of his sentence. It also reported he had behaved in a manner 'becoming his melancholy circumstances, and died in a truly penitent manner'.

Geddes was the last felon in Scotland to suffer for the crime and to be burnt following execution.

5

INDIAN PETER

Alexander Milne's map of Aberdeen in 1789 pinpoints the scene of a great scandal. 'The Old Barn where kidnapped boys were kept' stood in Renny's Wynd (modern Rennie's Court inherited the name) at the Green. Between 1740 and 1746, 600 youngsters, mostly boys, from the age of six upwards, were seized and shipped from Aberdeen to the Americas where they were sold into virtual slavery. The vile trade was called 'listing' to give it an air of respectability.

Aberdeen's kidnapping industry was not controlled by a gang of desperadoes but by a group of upright and respected officials and magistrates who paid agents to recruit youngsters either by bribery or force. Once in their clutches, the victims were imprisoned in the old barn or in houses in the Green or Torry, both of which were close to the shore where the human cargo was loaded on to a ship. They were also locked up in a cell in the tolbooth or in the House of Correction, founded in 1637 by Provost Jaffray, where minor offenders manufactured textiles.

The 'press gangs' ranged far and wide from the streets of the burgh. In *The Book of Bon Accord* (1839), local historian Joseph Robertson writes:

> The inhabitants of the neighbourhood dared not send their children into the town, and even trembled lest they should be snatched away from their homes. For in all parts of the county emissaries were abroad; in the dead of night children were taken by force from the beds where they slept; and the remote valleys of the Highlands, fifty miles distant from the city, were infested by ruffians who hunted their prey as beasts of the chase.

One teenage boy who caught their eye was Peter Williamson, who was born at a farm in the parish of Hirnlay, near Aboyne, in 1730, and who, at the age of ten, went to live with his aunt in Aberdeen. In January 1743, Peter, a strapping youngster, was playing on the quayside when approached by two men whom he later described as 'monsters of impiety'. They ignored the rules of indentured labour. Contracts had to be certified by a magistrate and minors had to have the permission of their parents. Peter was lured into the barn where the boys passed the time gambling, eating and drinking. A piper was hired either to entertain or deaden the sound of crying of the very young.

Their future was bleak and many committed suicide because of their treatment by the slave-masters in the Americas. The so-called 'kidnapping book', which was kept by the ringleaders in Aberdeen, carried the entry, 'To the man that brought Williamson: 1s 6d'. He was identified as James Smith, a local saddler, and he entertained prostitutes for his own pleasure, as this mind-boggling entry shows, 'To Colonel Horsie (*sic*) for his concubine: £1'!

The abducted children were allowed out of the barn to exercise on the shore or the Links. Three years before Peter was kidnapped, it was recorded that boys were kept in order 'while getting the air' by an overseer wielding a horsewhip which he did not hesitate to use. The villain was employed by John Burnet, a local merchant, who went by the soubriquet of 'Bonnie John'.

Peter's father, James Williamson, traced his son to the barn but was not allowed to make contact. By the time he returned with a warrant for Peter's release, he was too late. Peter had sailed for the New World on the *Planter* (other sources name the ship as the *Kenilworth*), under the command of Captain Robert Ragg, another local character who was implicated in the wicked trade.

Peter survived a stormy, eleven-week crossing of the Atlantic and the wrecking of the *Planter* in a raging gale off Cape May at the mouth of the Delaware. Ragg and his crew abandoned the youngsters to their fate but returned for the human cargo when the storm had abated. Peter was eventually landed at Philadelphia where he was sold for £16 for a term of seven years to Hugh Wilson, a fellow Scot who, in his youth, had been kidnapped in St Johnstown (Perth). Wilson proved a 'humane, worthy, honest man'. He had no children of his own and, when Peter, who could not read or write, expressed his willingness to go to school, his mentor agreed. For the next five years, Peter worked on the farm during the summer and attended school in winter, where he attained 'tolerable proficiency'. On his death, Peter's 'good master' left him the equivalent of £150 sterling, his best horse, saddle and his entire wardrobe. Peter was then seventeen.

A free man, with money in his pocket, he roamed the countryside for the next seven years doing jobbing work. Eventually he decided to settle down and wooed and wed a rich planter's daughter in Chester County, Pennsylvania. His father-in-law gifted Peter two hundred of acres of land on the Pennsylvania border, near the Forks of Delaware, in Berks County. Thirty acres of the land had already been cleared and a good house and a barn stood on it.

The future looked rosy for Peter and his wife. But their world was turned upside down when an undeclared war broke out in the early 1750s between Britain and France. The two colonial powers each had their respective Indian allies. However, the hostilities in North America were relegated to something of a sideshow when, following Britain's declaration of war on 18 May 1756, the conflict known as the Seven Years War erupted in Europe and elsewhere. On the night of 2 October 1754, while his wife was visiting relatives, a war party comprised of a dozen Indians loyal to the French, attacked their home. Peter was forced to surrender and, surprisingly, in light of the atrocities he later witnessed, his captors spared his life. The raiders torched the house and barn, destroying crops and livestock and made Peter carry their booty. Using him for this would perhaps explain why they kept him alive and, although they tortured him for their amusement, he lived to tell the tale.

During the time he was held prisoner, Peter studied his captors' dress, customs and barbaric methods of waging a guerrilla war against the British settlers. In one harrowing episode, Peter looked on helplessly as two of three white men, recaptured after escaping from his own captors, were hideously tortured with fire and red-hot irons, before being gutted alive. The third prisoner was buried up to his neck, scalped and a small fire was lit close to his head so that 'his eyes gushed out of their sockets.' Ironically, when the trio were first captured and brought to the camp, they told Peter how a trader had been roasted and eaten and his head turned into an 'Indian pudding'.

After three months in captivity, Peter managed to escape. His joyful homecoming was overshadowed by the news that his wife had died two months earlier. Peter gave a graphic account of his experiences to Governor Morris, who was satisfied enough to give him £3. The Scotsman's sworn affidavit was forwarded to the Assembly sitting at the State House and, soon after, Peter was summoned to Philadelphia to be interrogated by the speaker.

Peter turned his back on the soil and enlisted in the Pennsylvania Volunteers, part of a provincial force led by General William Shirley, the governor of Massachusetts. He became embroiled in further adventures which would have done justice to the pen of James Fenimore Cooper (1789–1851), author of ripping yarns, *The Last of the Mohicans*, *The Deerslayer* and *The Pathfinder*. In May 1848, *Blackwood's Magazine* claimed that Cooper was acquainted with Williamson's memoirs and might even have incorporated Peter's military experiences in his books.

In spring 1756, a war party attacked the Long family's plantation near Boston and massacred the couple and their servants and burned their property. The Indians carried off the dead couple's son and daughter and, when news reached Boston, the indefatigable Peter joined a 100-strong rescue party, led by Captain James Crawford, Miss Long's sweetheart. The militia overtook and slaughtered the Indians. They found Miss Long tied naked to a tree. She was alive but her brother had been tortured to death. Crawford and Miss Long were married soon after and Peter and his comrades were present.

One night during the Niagara Campaign in October 1755, he escaped drowning when a flat-bottomed boat used for transporting troops was smashed to bits by dangerous rapids on the River Onondaga. He pulled himself on to a bank where he was found next morning, 'in a wretched condition, quite benumbed, and almost dead with cold, having nothing on but [his] shirt'. He was sent to recuperate in hospital in Albany.

But Peter soon rejoined the fray and, when a French Canadian army, commanded by General Montcalm, laid siege to Fort Oswego on Lake Ontario, the intrepid Scot was one of the defenders. He was taken prisoner when Oswego fell in August 1756. The victors pillaged the fort and slaughtered the wounded. Peter, who received a serious hand wound in the action, was eventually repatriated to Plymouth, England, where he was discharged as unfit for duty and received a gratuity of six shillings.

Short of cash by the time he reached York, he persuaded a local business-man to sponsor the publication of his memoirs, grandly entitled, *French and Indian Cruelty: Exemplified in the Life and Various Vicissitudes of Fortune of Peter Williamson etc.* The book was dedicated to the British statesman William Pitt. A later edition carried a portrait of the author in war paint and wearing the dress, feathered headdress and all, of a Delaware Indian. Peter had an eye for publicity. Whenever he hawked his book he would don his war paint and tribal costume, carry a tomahawk and musket and smoke a 'peace pipe'. For good measure he would break into a war dance and release blood-curdling whoops. The book sold a total of 1750 copies in York and Newcastle and made him a handsome profit of more than £30.

In June 1758, Peter Williamson arrived back in Aberdeen in search of his long lost relatives – and additional book sales. He created a sensation in the Castlegate. In his memoirs, Peter lifted the lid on the 'villainous and execrable practice' of kidnapping. The town's bailies (magistrates) and merchants were in no hurry to smoke a 'peace pipe', however, and Peter was arrested, thrown in the tolbooth and charged with uttering 'a scurrilous and infamous libel on the corporation and city of Aberdeen'. He was forced to sign a statement denying his accusations against the civic officials or face imprisonment. He was also fined ten shillings and banished from the town. The offensive pages of his autobiography were torn out and burned at the Mercat Cross by the public hangman, watched by the town officers. (In the 1750s, the 'hangie' publicly burned a copy of the *Aberdeen Journal*, in which James Smith, the saddler who procured Peter Williamson, made a libellous statement against a former Lord Provost regarding the high price of meal and, in 1795, the hangman consigned Sandy 'Statio' Ross's peep-show to a bonfire.)

But the bold Indian fighter and great survivor had a score to settle. He would later complain of the 'very barbarous usage and ill treatment' he received in Aberdeen and in Edinburgh lawyers agreed to take up his case against the Aberdeen magistrates. In 1762 the Court of Session awarded him £100 damages plus £80 expenses. The court ruled that the defenders should be personally liable and that no burden be placed upon the town of Aberdeen. The wily magistrates managed to evade the decree of the court by paying the damages and costs from the Common Good Fund, which had its origins in Robert the Bruce's gift of the Stocket Forest to the burgh. According to Aberdeen historian Joseph Robertson:

> It was the intention of the officers of the crown to institute a criminal prosecution against the parties engaged in the trade of kidnapping, but it unfortunately happened that the wretches were secured from punishment by a certain Act of Indemnity.

After his courtroom victory, Peter raised an action for £1000 damages against his abductors, a group of respected citizens, which included Bailie William Fordyce, merchant, and former burgh treasurer, his father-in-law and town clerk depute Walter Cochran and Alexander Mitchell of Colpna. But the defenders persuaded Peter's lawyers that the case could be settled by arbitration in Aberdeen, without the costly intervention of the Court of Session. The arbitrator was the sheriff substitute of Aberdeenshire, James Forbes of Shiels, who was a heavy drinker, a weakness which both parties hoped to exploit – otherwise, if a decision was not reached by a certain date, the case would go back to the Court of Session.

Two days before the deadline Forbes was wined and dined around the clock. Peter got a friend to waylay Forbes by offering to buy him drink. He found the sheriff substitute downing hot punch in a tavern at 11 a.m. That Friday night, all three had a lively dinner in the New Inn, the Castle Street hostelry, where Dr Samuel Johnson, his biographer James Boswell and Robert Burns would later stay. During the boozy evening they drank 'helter-skelter' (the equivalent of binge drinking) until near midnight when the drunken Forbes was carried home by two maidservants and put to bed. Next morning a bleary-eyed Forbes was spirited away by a friend of the merchants to Archie Campbell's 'howff' where his hosts had rented an entire floor and orders were given that they should not be disturbed. They spent the rest of the day gambling and drinking claret, Malaga, punch, porter and, oh, yes, tea and coffee!

Before staggering off to bed, the sheriff substitute ruled in favour of the kidnappers. The decree was read aloud on the Plainstones next morning, as churchgoers hurried past. Peter complained to the Court of Session, who overturned Forbes' decision. On 3 December 1768, five years after the Seven Years War ended in a British victory, he was awarded £200 damages and costs of 100 guineas (£105).

Peter Williamson made his home in Edinburgh, where he married, more than once, and raised a family. He wrote several versions of his experiences in America. As well as being a successful writer, he was a tavern keeper, publisher, printer, postmaster and inventor. 'Indian Peter', as he was known, opened a popular tavern in Old Parliament Close at St Giles. The signboard proclaimed, 'Peter Williamson, Vintner from the other World'. The 'other World' was a reference to his globetrotting activities. Magistrates would gather in the tavern to partake of the 'deid-chack', a dinner that they held at the expense of the city, after attending a public execution. It was said Bailie James Torry grew so impatient of one culprit's long-winded prayers and psalm-singing on the scaffold, he whispered to a fellow magistrate, 'I wish he would be done; that knuckle of veal will be roasted to a cinder!' Lord Provost Creech abandoned the practice.

Peter also owned a coffee house in the Parliament Hall, which was frequented by Court of Session lawyers and journalists. The poet Robert Fergusson immortalised the latter establishment in 'The Rising of the Session':

> This vacance is a heavy doom
> On Indian Peter's coffee-room,
> For a' his china pigs are toom;
> Nor do we see
> In wine the sucker biskets soom
> As light's a flee.

(Note: 'China pigs' were stone bottles, 'toom' meant empty, a 'sucker bisket' was a biscuit topped with sugar and 'soom' meant swim or float.)

Peter's other accomplishments ranged from the invention of a reaping machine and the establishment of the capital's first Penny Post, for which he received a pension, to publishing a weekly newspaper, *The Scots Spy*, and the first Edinburgh street directory. His wife, Jean, whom he divorced, and his daughter were nimble-fingered, making everything from silk gloves to shrouds. Peter died on 19 January 1799, in his sixty-ninth year, and was buried in the Old Calton graveyard.

6

GREAT ESCAPES

Rings of airn and bolts of steel
Fell like ice frae hand and heel!

Sir Walter Scott

Fate smiled on the gypsy rogue Peter Young, the eighteenth-century equivalent of Houdini, as he waited to keep a date with the Aberdeen hangman. Tradition had it that he has escaped from every jail in Scotland and some swore there wasn't a prison built that could hold him. Indeed, when he was led back to his cell in the tolbooth after being sentenced to death, he boasted to jailers that 'the hemp was not grown that would hang him'. On the night of 24 October 1787, the wily Peter, sometimes called Patrick, finalised plans for a daring mass breakout with his wife, her mother and six other prisoners.

The tolbooth – the so-called 'Mids o' Mar' – had been a gloomy depository of the guilt and misery of Aberdeen and its shire since it was built in 1629 to replace a second one built on the same spot during the reign of King Robert III. A much earlier twelfth-century tolbooth had stood closer to the harbour. Although present-day visitors to the tolbooth, now the city's Museum of Civic History, might find it hard to believe that anyone could have escaped from there, its cells were not escape-proof. In 1638, Alexander Keith of Balmuir, a debtor, was smuggled out in a trunk and fled to his castle at Boddam, near Peterhead. Viscount Frendraught escaped by a similar method and, in

1675, Francis Irvine of Hilton and other debtors caused 'affront and abuse' to the burgh when they smashed their way out of a cell in the upper storey and clambered down a rope to freedom. The jailers faced the wrath of the magistrates.

In 1698, the civic fathers tightened regulations that had allowed certain prisoners to leave the jail as long as they made a speedy return. Unfortunately, James Gordon, a brother of the Laird of Arradoul, walked out of the front door at noon after getting his captors hopelessly drunk and failed to return. Their negligence led to humiliation in the stocks, imprisonment on bread and water and banishment with their wives and families. The more trustworthy George Forbes was handed the job and given the title, 'Goodman of the Tolbooth'.

In 1749, two condemned culprits cheated the hangman by escaping. Aberdeen butcher Alexander Macdonald's accomplice in murder, Alex Philp, was hanged. But, the day before his execution, Macdonald and George Burnett, who was confined on horse theft, were aided in their flight by two women and a man who loosened their irons. Burnett was eventually recaptured and banished. Macdonald got clean away. In the same year, William Wilson, a robber from Fyvie, broke free as he was escorted back to the jail after being sentenced to death at the Circuit Court next door. He fled down nearby Luxembourg Court in Castle Street and was never seen or heard of again. Their jailer, Alexander Thomson, clung to his job for another five years before he and two assistants were sacked for allowing a rapist, Alexander Irvine, an Echt shoemaker, to make a break for freedom. Irvine was recaptured and forced into service in the Royal Navy.

The Aberdeen magistrates were familiar with Young's jail-busting reputation and were determined he would become the first criminal to be hanged on new gallows erected at the door of the tolbooth. How did he acquire his formidable reputation? Peter was born to the life of a 'caird' (itinerant tinker) at Mergie, on the Slug Road, north-west of Stonehaven. He was the son of James or Alexander Young – 'Caird' Young – and Ann Graham, whose brother was the 'king' of the Scottish gypsies. Charles Graham, nicknamed 'Gle'ed' because of a squint eye, came from Lochgelly in Fife. He had succeeded John Gun, a notorious cattle thief mentioned by Sir Walter Scott in *The Lady of the Lake*, who was transported to Virginia in 1754 after his death sentence was commuted for theft at the Michael Fair of Kinkell, Perthshire. Ann bore 'Caird' Young three brawny sons, Robert, Peter and John. Although John was almost six feet tall, his mother described him as 'the dwarf o' a' [her] bairns'. Peter and his brothers were introduced to crime at an early age. He stole chickens by fishing for them with crooked pins baited with breadcrumbs. He was good with his hands – small neat hands which one day would enable him to slip out of handcuffs – and made horn-craft and mended pots and pans. He was also taught the most efficient method of cutting iron bars and picking locks. Peter struggled with writing but, as a youth, he picked up the skill of making 'chouries' – saw knives – which, time and again, allowed him to cut through shackles and the bars of his cell.

His first attempt at crime ended in dismal failure when, after breaking into a farmhouse at Tough on Donside, he was caught and soundly thrashed. He joined forces with his brother, Robert, and their reputation induced country folk to have a word in the ear of an army sergeant recruiting for Lord Strathaven. But they gave the sergeant the slip and switched their operations to the wild and desolate hills and moors of the Cabrach. They repaid a sheep farmer who gave them employment and lodgings by burgling his house and stealing bedding and goods. They were caught and sent to the 'Mids o' Mar' where their strapping build caught the eye of an army captain engaged in raising a company. He decided jail was the safest place for his new recruits until he was ready to march. The brothers had other ideas. They faked scurvy by smearing their legs with paste and were transferred to the infirmary. That same night, they escaped by jumping from a second-floor window although there was a guard on the door. The jailers found the fake paste and a large bolt hole at the back of the chimney in their cell.

Peter parted company with Robert and fled to England where, in league with another rogue, he plundered a rich man's house near York and stole silver plate. Before he returned to his homeland at the age of eighteen, Peter would pack a lot of adventure into his short life, including fighting for opposing sides in the American War of Independence. He sailed from England in a privateer which was captured soon after leaving the English Channel by an American frigate. Peter and his shipmates were taken to Boston where he enlisted in Washington's Light Horse. He deserted, taking with him his horse, arms and an officer's uniform he had found in a tent. He reached British lines and joined Colonel Tarleton's legion. He fell into American hands a second time but he was not recognised as a deserter. In Boston, he was locked up with other British prisoners – but not for long. After fashioning 'chouries', he hacked his way out of their cell and led them to freedom.

The fugitives boarded a brigantine, deserted and moored in a creek, and weighed anchor. They had scant knowledge of seamanship but luckily fell in with a Royal Navy frigate which escorted them to Halifax in Nova Scotia. The captured ship was sold and the prize money divided amongst the escapers. Peter later joined a line-of-battle ship and served as a seaman for a year. A fall from the yardarm left a deep scar on his temple, a distinguishing mark that would cost him dearly.

On returning to England, he resorted to his old ways. Before he deserted, he had borrowed money from the purser 'to relieve his poor parents'. He joined a privateer 'to cruise against the Dutch' and was taken prisoner. He and the rest of the crew were held at a fortress but, yet again, he managed to break out. This time he scaled an eighteen-foot-high wall with the aid of knotted blankets and swam the moat. None of his fellow prisoners had the courage to follow. He swam a broad river and eventually reached Ostende, where he was taken onboard a vessel bound for the Firth of Forth.

Back in Scotland, Peter joined forces with his uncle, 'Gle'ed' Graham, in Lochgelly. There he met and fell in love with Jean Wilson, whose father, James Brown, had been hanged with an accomplice in Edinburgh in the autumn of 1733. Jean was the same age as Peter and adept at picking pockets, thanks to the tuition of her mother, Margaret Brown, and her aunt, Agnes Brown, the wife of 'Gle'ed' Graham.

Peter and Jean were cousins and became common-law husband and wife before setting out on a trail of crime in north-east Scotland. Posing as cattle-dealers at principal markets, they reaped rich pickings through thieving. Their accomplices drew a large crowd by arranging a sham fight. When a purse or pocketbook was stolen, it was instantly handed to a partner in crime. The couple were arrested more than twenty times but the law was unable to implicate them. However, Peter's luck seemed to have run out when he was eventually arrested at Charlestown of Aboyne. But he fled by jumping clean over the heads of spectators from the topmost outer stairs of the 'thieves' hole' (the village lock-up). He got away from Brechin tolbooth after cutting a bar from the cell window and the turnkey at Stonehaven almost lost his job after his famous prisoner picked a lock and rejoined his gang.

In the middle of 1786, he and his cronies, including Agnes Brown, were locked up in Perth jail on housebreaking charges. But soon the gang was on the run again. In May 1787, the cairds, along with Robert Young, gathered at the Greencairns of Balbegno, Kincardineshire, where they arranged to rendezvous at Aberdeen on 1 June, when large crowds were expected for the hanging of William Webster, an ex-soldier and vagrant, who turned to housebreaking and theft after being banished for life from his home town of Aberdeen for operating a crooked wheel-of-fortune game. One of the stolen items, a gown belonging to a fourteen-year-old girl, was produced in court. The owner failed to identify the garment. As some time had elapsed since the theft, Webster believed she had grown in size and the gown would no longer fit. He insisted she try it on. But, when the teenager pulled it on, she recognised a stain which was later said to have been a spot of blood caused when she accidentally pricked herself with a needle. Webster had gambled once too often.

At Webster's hanging, the last to be held in the Market Place, a great number of onlookers had their pockets picked. Agnes Brown was arrested. She was transported for seven years after being flogged through the streets. (Shop-breaker James Grant or Glass made local criminal history on 27 June 1788 when he was the first to be executed on new gallows at the door of the tolbooth. 'The place on which the criminal stood was made to fall down, and leave him suspended,' it was reported. It was an English invention.)

Peter and Jean fled on horseback to Banffshire, with a large brown dog for company. After robbing a shop in Portsoy, the law closed in on Jean and the 'braw gentleman wi' a bonnie buckle in his hat'. The couple were arrested and hauled before the magistrates at Turriff. They pleaded ignorance of the charges but the dog inadvertently betrayed them as its description had been circulated in their wanted notices. They were taken to Banff prison but the pair promptly made a break for freedom in broad daylight. Peter was cornered in a blind alley but Jean reached Turriff on a stolen horse. On learning her husband was again under lock and key, she expressed sadness that Peter had been 'ta'en before he got awa' the length o' his leg'.

The Banff magistrates were wary of their prisoner's jail-breaking reputation. A round-the-clock guard was mounted and Peter was fettered with heavy leg irons, as thick as a man's wrist. Peter produced his faithful 'chouries' and sawed through his restraints. He concealed his handiwork by binding his legs with rags on the excuse the irons chaffed his skin. He planned to make a break for it while being escorted back to Aberdeen. But the ploy backfired and he was bound hard with ropes. By this time, Jean had been recaptured and the couple stood at the bar at the Aberdeen Autumn Circuit Court in 1787, where they were found guilty of robbery and condemned to hang. Jean pleaded that she was seven months' pregnant but a medical examination showed she was only a short time gone. Her sentence stood although the date of her execution was postponed until 9 August 1788.

Peter's execution was scheduled for 16 November 1787 and strict measures were instigated in the Aberdeen tolbooth. His legs were manacled to the 'lang gade or gad', a thick iron bar fixed to the floor of his cell. A guard was posted under the windows of the jail every night and fetters and very narrow handcuffs were specially made for Peter. No one was allowed to see the very important prisoner unless accompanied by a jailer. Fortunately for Peter the head turnkey, Andrew Gray, was incompetent and would later be accused of being 'guilty of great negligence and inattention to his duties'. Gray allowed street pedlars to enter the jail to sell porter, ale and spirits to the prisoners (liquor was sold in Scottish prisons until the middle of the nineteenth century). He entrusted the keys of the prison, day and night, to a poor servant who, for a few coppers, allowed anyone off the street to peer at the prisoners.

It is little wonder that on the first night in captivity Peter was heard tampering with his fetters. A search revealed saw knives hidden in the chimney of his cell. But Peter seemed resigned to his impending doom and requested the benefit of a clergyman to attend to his spiritual needs. One evening, as the head turnkey was examining the bars of the death cell, Peter commented, 'Aye, aye, Mister Gray. I winna come oot now till I come oot at the door.' Gray understood this to refer to Peter's last walk to the gallows. But the debonair rogue had other ideas.

Unknown to Gray, the illiterate Peter arranged with an assistant jailer for three fellow prisoners, James Memis, a watchmaker-turned-thief, and housebreaker John Monro, an infamous thief, both from Johnshaven, and Paddy Burns, to take turns in reading the Bible to him behind a locked door. He, in turn, initiated the trio into the mysteries of dealing with stubborn locks and fetters. They managed to free Peter from his handcuffs and cut the rivets of his leg irons, although he took great care to wear them in the presence of a jailer. After sawing through a window stanchion, they disguised the break with grease and rust.

Meal sellers at the back of the tolbooth warned Gray that attempts were being made to cut the bars and handed him a 'chourie' that had dropped on their heads. Blacksmiths checked the bars of the windows but found nothing to arouse suspicions. Peter and his accomplices chose eight o'clock on the night of 24 October to make their legendary escape. After they broke out of their cells on the upper floor, they planned to release Peter's wife, Jean, and her light-fingered aunt, Agnes, who had yet to face a whipping and transportation after her arrest at William Webster's execution. They were in the cell below. The men silently picked locks, slid back bolts and forced their way through an iron door, an oak door and other cells as well as an iron yett (a gate of interwoven bars). They accomplished the task, not without bullying from Peter, by brute force and resourcefulness, utilising everything from an old nail to force back feather springs to red-hot spikes to burn round the locks of the iron-bound doors (the massive padlocks can be seen in the city's Marischal and Tolbooth Museums).

After releasing the two women, they padded bare-footed into the street as the guard changed out of sight. It was three in the morning of 25 October. The escapers were Peter Young, his wife Jean, Agnes Brown, John Paul, who was under sentence of death for sheep-stealing, Paddy Burns, William Bartlet, a soldier who had shot a man dead in a quarrel, Patrick Anderson, a boy facing transportation, James Memis and John Monro. The daring jailbreak was not discovered for another three hours by which time the escapers headed in the westerly direction of the rolling hills and forests of Deeside. Peter, ever the humanitarian, carried the ailing Memis for several miles on his back.

After lurking in the hills and caves around Peter's birthplace at Mergie, the fugitives were spotted descending the hills north of Laurencekirk in the Mearns and then heading for the Mill of Kincardine, the home of a coarse character who befriended criminals. The laird of Phesdo, Sir Edward Bannerman, led a party of lawmen and servants to the mill but, as they closed in, Peter and Anderson slipped out of a back window, while the rest of the escapers were arrested and taken back to Aberdeen. Sir Edward was reported to have stumbled on the point of shooting the elusive caird or so it was said.

Aberdeen magistrates posted a reward of twenty guineas for Peter's capture while a 'handsome reward' was offered for Anderson who was picked up the following January. The official proclamation has left a detailed and startling description of Peter:

> A stout (strong) young man, pockpitted, aged about twenty-two, with a remarkably sharp eye, about five feet ten inches high, thin-made, has an arch-sneering look, is a native of Deeside, in the county of Aberdeen, the language of which county he speaks.

Peter was wearing 'a tartan short jacket of large squares or lozens (diamond-shapes), trowsers of the same stuff, and a bonnet, so that he is rather a remarkable figure'. Oddly, there was no mention of his scar. Peter probably spoke Gaelic as well as English – the old tongue was still being spoken in some Deeside glens into the early nineteenth century.

Peter roamed the hills and glens of Angus but later denied he had been spotted in Aberdeen disguised in woman's clothes, although it was suggested he had returned to the burgh with the aim of freeing his wife and fellow compatriots who were back inside the tolbooth. In December, he turned up in Perth where he was a hunted man. The previous year he had broken out of jail there after being arrested for breaking into a church with others and stealing the pewter baptism basin, mistaking it for silver. The thieves stripped the kirk of its green velvet cloth and, from Lord Kinnoul's loft, they took purple velvet chair covers. Always the exhibitionist, Peter fashioned a handsome jacket of pulpit cloth, which he trimmed with fringes, and a vest from the chair covers. He created sensation when he appeared at market in this bizarre apparel.

Peter was reunited with 'Gle'ed' Graham and they headed for Aberdeen in the hope of rescuing their spouses. However, they got no further than Arbroath where they were arrested for committing two burglaries. Peter gave the investigating sheriff a false name but a gentleman recognised him by the scar on his temple. Peter and his uncle were clapped in the stocks in the iron room of the local jail to await an escort from Aberdeen. By the time the officer arrived in Arbroath, both prisoners had fled. During the night, they had complained of the cold and had been shifted to a cell with a fire. By morning, they had vanished. They would later claim they had bribed the jailer to let them go.

But the net was tightening. Despite deep snowdrifts, the fugitives got as far as the Bridge of Dun, near Brechin, where the sheriff's men rode them down. Graham was quickly overpowered. Peter, who was still wearing handcuffs, dived into a snow-wreathed ditch only to be found by a pursuer's dog.

On New Year's Day 1788, a huge crowd milled around outside the Aberdeen tolbooth to catch a glimpse of the remarkable Peter Young arrive by post-chaise from Arbroath. His arms and legs were pinioned and he was accompanied by soldiers. The jailer Gray was sacked for his incompetence and a more vigilant head turnkey appointed. The prison had been made more secure since the great escape. The bars in the window were replaced, the flagstones in the cells checked and relaid and a fingertip search was conducted for saw knives. Peter was strip-searched and kept in solitary confinement in a damp, airless and unheated room, which drew complaints from two doctors who feared for his life. He was eventually moved to a cell with a fireplace.

Never-say-die Peter was handed a further opportunity to flee justice. A decently dressed woman delivered a jug of broth to the prison. The jug also held six shoemaker's paring knives, fashioned into files. But, before he could cut himself free, a messenger arrived from Edinburgh with orders to take him to the capital. As he left the tolbooth, his wife, Jean, who would be transported instead of being hanged, cried out, 'O, Peter, Peter! You should hae hidden oot o' their grips when you was oot o' their grips. I'll never see you again!'

If Aberdeen had its 'Mids o' Mar', the capital boasted 'The Heart of Midlothian', the gloomy and loathsome Edinburgh Tolbooth, next to St Giles Cathedral in the High Street. On arrival Peter was chained to the 'lang gade' but, within an hour, the turnkey surprised him attempting to cut through a leg iron with a saw knife. A body search revealed two more 'chouries' hidden in the inner sole of his shoe.

The celebrated caird was not in the least over-awed by the majesty of the law when he appeared at the High Court of Justiciary in Edinburgh on 3 March 1788. Asked by Lord Justice Clerk if he had anything to say about why the former sentence of death imposed on him in Aberdeen the previous year should not go ahead, Peter replied, 'I am not the man.' Peter's counsel, Charles Hope (the judge who condemned Gillan, the Stynie Moor murderer) argued that, as the prisoner denied his identity, it was his right as a British subject to have the question tried by a jury, as it was a question of fact and not a point of law. The case was adjourned and, after eleven days, the bench of six judges ruled no jury was required. The next day, William Stewart, who was the mace bearer at the Autumn Circuit in Aberdeen in 1787, and Alexander Guthrie, the Circuit Clerk, swore to the prisoner's identity, pointing to the telltale scar.

Peter was sentenced to death – but his execution was postponed until Wednesday 2 July 1788. Alert to his escapades, a special 'cage' – actually a square-shaped box of plate iron – was built for him within his cell, situated above the hall in the tolbooth. (There is an echo here of the fictional Hannibal 'The Cannibal' Lecter's confinement.) Six days before his execution Peter sent his wife a lock of his hair with a letter dictated to a priest or turnkey:

> I hope in God you will get liberty: if you do, I hope you will take care and keep it. When you are brought to bed, if you have a son, I desire you will call him after me: and if you get liberty, and the child and you are spared together, I hope you will do your endeavour to bring it up in an honest way. My dear, what could a man do more than lay down his life to save his wife's? For in coming to save yours I lost my own.

Peter's executioner was 'Jock Heich', a thief in his own right. On the day he was hanged on gallows erected on the roof of a railed extension at the west end of the Edinburgh tolbooth, Peter's wife gave birth to their daughter. Peter Young was twenty-four years old. His brother John, as we already know (see Chapter One), ended his days 'facing doon Marischal Street' when he was hanged by Robbie Welsh in 1801 for the murder of his cousin, Hugh Graham. There is no record of the fate of their eldest brother, Robert, although it was said that, when their mother, Ann Graham, was asked about her sons, she would reply sorrowfully, 'They're a' hanged.' Jean Wilson was locked up in the Aberdeen tolbooth till June 1791, four years after her trial, after which she was sent to London for transportation to New South Wales.

A week after Peter was executed, a dramatic bid by his former accomplices, Burns, Bartlet and Anderson, to escape from the Aberdeen tolbooth by tunnelling through a cell wall was foiled by vigilant jailers. The prisoners, who awaited transportation, were then confined in the stocks in another room. They broke out of the stocks and used the wooden device to barricade the cell which they then wrecked. They attacked the under-jailer and it took military guards to overpower them. They were put into their original cell and 'properly ironed'.

Their cronies, Monro and Memis, were found guilty of theft and housebreaking at the Spring Circuit Court at Aberdeen in June 1788 and were flogged through the streets and banished from the county for life. Monro, alias John Stewart, was arrested for housebreaking at Cairnbulg and, as a result of fellow criminals perjuring themselves at his trial, walked to the gallows declaring his innocence. On being pressed by a clergyman to confess or go to Hell, he replied that there were 'many coot shentlemens there'.

There is an amusing story, most likely apocryphal, that, after prisoners had fled the Aberdeen tolbooth, a witty felon had scrawled 'Rooms to Rent' on the front door. But equally farcical situations arose elsewhere. The sheriff in Elgin was about to hold court when he was told not to bother as all the prisoners had walked out. On the recapture of some of the culprits, they were brought to Inverness to appear before a judge. But the jailer had gone to the country taking the only key of the prison with him. In 1701, the Elgin tolbooth was set alight by a distraught prisoner. Eleven years after this, prisoners attempted to break out of Banff jail by burning the cell doors. The town council ordered the doors to be sheathed in iron and gave the job to a rural blacksmith as the local smith's quotation was too high.

In 1767, along the coast at Cullen, the tolbooth was in a sad need of repair. The walls were weak and damp and the outer door rotten and useless while the inner door 'was not fit for a prison'. The iron window grates, it was reported, could easily be forced out and prisoners had access to the roof, which was rotten. In 1723, a thief, T. Reid, escaped from the Cullen tolbooth by raising the 'daill (plank) at the foot of the door with his hands', allowing him to 'crap oot from below the door'. On his recapture, he stood in jougs for six hours every day before being locked up in a bid to find out who was his accomplice in crime. Once back in jail, his arms were pinioned and he was sat in the stocks. Somehow, he freed himself and got out of the stocks before escaping by the same method as before. He lurked about the town for three days before being recaptured. He was imprisoned, tied up and put back in the stocks. This time there was no escape. Four guards took turns at night to watch him. He was finally banished from Banffshire and warned that, if he returned, 'death would be inflicted on him without process of the law'.

In 1817, the famous author Sir Walter Scott could be found poking around the ruins of the newly demolished tolbooth in Edinburgh. 'The Heart of Midlothian' was no more. Robert Johnston, the Dean of Guild, procured for him the carved stones from the prison gateway, together with the door and padlock, which was sent to Abbotsford, Scott's home above the Tweed. Rubble was used for the construction of drains and sewers in the vicinity of the Fettes Row, which became the 'grave of the old Tolbooth'.

But whatever happened to 'The Cage'? Seven years after it was demolished, Robert Chambers, publisher and author, gave a graphic description of the tolbooth and its cell within a cell – the box of plate iron 'said to have been constructed for the purpose of confining some extraordinary culprit who had broken half the jails in the kingdom'. Chambers did not identify the culprit but his words might have given some comfort to Peter Young who boasted there was not a jail built that could hold him.

A day or so after Peter was brought to Aberdeen from Arbroath the north-east burgh had a second 'unusual guest', according to the *Aberdeen Journal*:

In the forenoon a hare came down the Gallowgate, Broadgate, across the Plainstones, and up the Castlegate, and tho' chased by dogs and boys without number, run out at the Justice port, into the garden grounds, and got clear off.

Peter would have loved that!

The East Prison in Lodge Walk, built in 1829 to replace the old tolbooth jail next door, was the scene of a dramatic breakout by five prisoners who had been transferred from the city's Bridewell, or West Prison, to await trial on housebreaking and theft charges at the next Circuit Court. At 6 a.m. on Wednesday 20 April 1825, Coutts and two brothers named Stirling smashed through their cell wall with an iron crowbar smuggled to them by accomplices within the jail. The crowbar had been drawn up on the end of a cord from the cell below. Using spring-saws, they then freed five prisoners by cutting the chains that secured their cell door. They lifted massive stones set in an upper floor then dropped eight feet on to the ceiling which formed the roof of the courthouse. They tunnelled through the ceiling and lowered themselves by knotted blankets to the floor. They easily overcame the next obstacle – two large windows facing Lodge Walk. But, as they scrambled outside, the courthouse keeper raised the alarm and some would-be escapers were held back. In Castle Street, astonished passengers waiting to board the stagecoach at the New Inn watched as two prisoners, Alexander Stirling and Coutts, were overpowered. One was wrestled to the ground by Simon Grant, a well-known law officer. But three of the fugitives, John McLaren (36), a Dundee weaver with experience of the sea, Joseph McDonald (23), a Peterhead whale-fisherman, and William Stirling (20), an Aberdeen cooper, were never caught.

The Bridewell or West Prison, which opened in 1809, straddled the north end of present-day Rose Street. The lofty building, its gardens and exercise yard were enclosed by a 14-foot-high wall and its upkeep was shared between town and county. It was modelled on other bridewells where prisoners were paid for menial tasks. But it wasn't a home from home and, in June 1831, Irishman Robert Gallie, who was two months into a year's hard labour for housebreaking and theft, made his break for freedom. He had cut a hole in his third-floor cell door with a chisel, which he had been given to repair a weaving loom, and got into the lobby. By forcing the lock of the lobby door and lifting flagstones, he eventually reached the ground floor by lowering himself down through ventilators. He was unable to force the outer iron door and waited till turnkey John Barnett unlocked it. The governor, W. R. Chalmers, rushed in from the garden and, though injured in the subsequent struggle, helped overpower Gallie, who was placed in irons.

The Bridewell was pulled down in 1869 and is now a bare memory caught in sketches and faded photographs. It disappeared along with the horse-drawn 'Rose Street omnibus', which transported prisoners between the East and West jails. The gap site was filled for a brief time by a pleasure garden and recreation grounds. The Highland games champion Donald Dinnie performed there. Aberdeen advocate Lachlan Mackinnon attended the inaugural fête in his schooldays and thrilled at the antics of 'The Man Fish' in a glass tank of water.

7

'POOR RITCHIE'

In 1818, people stood at the foot of the walls of the Aberdeen tolbooth to collect slips of paper dropped from a cell window. The 'little billets' were allegedly penned or dictated by James Ritchie, 'whose youthful and comely' appearance had captured the imagination of the town, if not the whole of north-east Scotland. In some quarters, it was whispered he was revered as a saint rather than a criminal about to be hanged at the age of only seventeen, a birthday that passed while he awaited trial at the Spring Circuit Court. In the days leading up to his execution, the notes, which admitted the folly of his ways and urged people not to follow in his footsteps, showered down from his cell on the upper floor. The local clergy – 'his dear instructors' – most certainly had a hand in these pathetic epistles.

Ritchie's crime was the theft of thirty sheep from the parks at Gordon Castle, Fochabers, the home of Alexander, Fourth Duke of Gordon, whose beautiful wife, it was said, raised the Gordon Highlanders by offering each new recruit a shilling and a kiss. It was believed the boy had been the 'dupe of adroit thieves'. Ritchie had never before been in trouble but, at his trial, the jury found him guilty with an earnest recommendation of mercy. However, because of the frequency of the crime in the region, sheep-stealers and horse-thieves could expect little or no mercy.

There is a curious footnote to the case of William Burnett, of Strachan, Kincardineshire, who was hanged in Aberdeen on 31 October 1783 for stealing a mare and an ox. After the theft, a farmer came by Burnett who was fast asleep by the roadside. The man recognised the animals and had the culprit brought into Aberdeen the same day. The author of *The Black Kalendar of Aberdeen* (1871) commented:

> It has, with the country people, always been deemed unlucky to have a hand in bringing offenders to justice, and this opinion would, no doubt, often effect its own confirmation. The man who apprehended Burnett, it is stated, never afterwards throve a single day, but came to great poverty, having, it is said, last been seen carrying coals in Aberdeen; and, it is added, that during his destitution he often regretted having meddled with a matter which did not concern him.

Burnett was the first felon to be hanged in the Market Place (Castlegate) since Morison was gibbeted at the Gallow Hill in 1776.

Some accused of the crime of sheep-stealing would rather take their own life than face the gallows. In July 1751, William Still, a butcher, was under lock and key in Strathbogie before being brought for trial in Aberdeen next day, when, according to the gallows humour of an *Aberdeen Journal* writer, 'in order to save the trouble of a long journey, and the tedious process of a long trial, he hanged himself in his garters, yesterday morning'.

Around the same time that Ritchie was arrested in January 1818, James Grant, a Kincardineshire man, was detained for having stolen sheep from a farm at Bridge of Dye, on the Cairn o' Mount road, and selling them at Montrose. He was locked up in the Stonehaven tolbooth, prior to his appearance at the Circuit Court in Aberdeen in April. But, as he was being conveyed by cart over the Brig o' Dee, he eluded his escort and hurled himself over the parapet to be 'dashed to pieces' below. The *Aberdeen Chronicle* remarked, 'He made an example of himself as impressive as if he had suffered in our market place.' Grant's suicide was to have a bearing on Ritchie's fate.

Bizarre punishments were inflicted on cattle thieves. The *Aberdeen Journal* of 9 January 1753 reported that:

> On Saturday, Alexander Martin, tenant, in Westertown of Huntly, was brought to this city, and incarcerated in the tolbooth, by a warrant from the Sheriff, for stealing and slaughtering an ox, the

property of William Anderson, in Cairntown of Cowburty. He was wrapped in the ox-hide by way of a great-coat, with the horns properly placed.

On 17 May 1751, sheep-stealers William Macdonald and his wife, Elspet Grant, were paraded through the town with two sheepskins hung around their necks. Their hands were tied behind their backs and the common hangman walked behind them, holding the ropes. They were banished from the county and warned that, if they returned, they would be whipped and banished for a second time. But, unlike James Ritchie, they did not face the ultimate fate.

However, a wave of sympathy went out to the teenager when his background was made public in the days following his trial. He had been born on 9 April 1801 at Gardenstown (also known as Gamrie) on the ruggedly beautiful Banffshire coast. He was an orphan, his father having died when he was two and his mother dying when he was twelve. At thirteen, he worked as gardener for the Garden family of Troup, the people who founded Gamrie, but he left without warning. According to a report at the time of his execution, he ended up in London where he followed a 'sinful and vicious course of life' with the result that he and a fellow servant appeared before a court on a charge of theft but he was acquitted.

As Ritchie had a clean criminal sheet before the Gordon case, strenuous efforts were made to gain him a reprieve. People from all walks of local life – university professors, the clergy and members of the business community – got up petitions. The Duke of Gordon was approached but, in the beginning, he appeared to turn a deaf ear to their pleas to intercede.

Ritchie was due to keep his date with hangman Johnny Milne on Friday 5 June. During his time in the death cell, Ritchie constantly had a minister of religion at his ear. It was reported that he 'listened with much earnestness to the exhortations' of the clergymen of whom there were five in all: Rev. Mr Thom, the jail chaplain, Rev. Dr Brown, Rev. Dr Ross, Rev. James Kidd and Mr Valentine Ward of the Wesleyan Methodists.

Ritchie went to the gallows with a prayer on his lips. He made his appearance on the scaffold at the front door of the tolbooth five minutes after the clocks of the burgh had struck two. As was the macabre custom, he wore a shroud. The *Aberdeen Journal* said the youth 'maintained a composure and firmness superior to his years, exciting the astonishment of the very numerous spectators, who witnessed the revolting spectacle'. After a short prayer, Ritchie had a warning for the young people in the crowd – obey the laws of God and the precepts of religion and avoid Sabbath breaking and bad company. He then bowed to the clergymen, magistrates and spectators before stepping on to the drop, which fell at ten minutes to three. He died 'without a struggle'. The young lad's ordeal had lasted forty-five minutes.

Ritchie was given no respite by speechwriters. Copies of a broadsheet, headed *Last Speech, Confession and Dying Declaration* and embroidered with illustrations of an hourglass, skull and crossbones, were being sold by chapmen on the streets soon after the execution. Even as Ritchie's corpse swung like a tassel at the end of the rope, Rev. Ward took the opportunity to remind onlookers about the evils of Sabbath breaking. But, by now, the crowd, some in tears, had begun to drift away.

In 1927, author Louisa Innes Lumsden, said that one of her mother's earliest recollections was of the day of Ritchie's execution and of a crowd of people, mostly women, passing the gate of Springhill House, the family summer home, in 'great excitement' following the execution. 'There was great indignation at this execution and the cruelty of the law.' However, her mother's memory failed her. 'A man had been apprehended at the same time as the boy,' wrote Lumsden, 'and the two were being taken to prison in a cart, when the man sprang out, jumped over the bridge across the Denburn in Union Street and was killed.' She was obviously referring to Grant's suicide leap at the Brig o' Dee.

A war of words followed Ritchie's tragic death. The general feeling was that the elderly Duke of Gordon had not done enough to save the boy's neck. Critics recalled that a cattle thief, William Souter, son of Lord Halkerston's ground officer, was sentenced to hang in Aberdeen in July 1774 but he was pardoned because of his age (20) and banished to the plantations for life. The Duke of Gordon did make a last-minute effort to have Ritchie pardoned but his appeal to the Home Secretary failed. The government had been determined to make an example of Ritchie. Notice of the Duke's unsuccessful plea for mercy was contained in a letter which arrived in Aberdeen from London the day after the hanging.

Lewis Smith, an Aberdeen bookseller and stationer, left a graphic account of the execution in his unpublished memoirs. He pointed out that sheep-stealing had become so common the judges resolved 'to make an example of the first well authenticated case'. He believed that, if Grant had not committed suicide, *he* would have hanged and not 'poor Ritchie'. Writing in the late nineteenth century, Smith, who was fifteen at the time of the execution, said:

> Aberdeen went into mourning, shutting up places of business and going into the country to escape the exhibition that was to vindicate the majesty of the law, and deter offenders from breaking it in all future time. Although participating in the universal feeling of pity for the criminal my curiosity to see the tragedy was too strong to overcome and I witnessed the whole scene . . .
>
> The scaffold projected into Castle Street – the appearance upon it of the ruddy-faced innocent looking lad, in his graveclothes, and him yet living – the universal sigh that ran through the crowd when the chaplain began the devotional exercises (it was Mr. Thom, master of Gordon's Hospital who held the office) – the sobs that mingled with the singing of the psalm by the crowd – the kind large-hearted Professor Kidd, as he stood by him to the last, and the bustling movements of the executioner (John Milne himself a criminal), the step upon the Drop, the bang when it fell and the cries that would be held no longer, left an impression on my mind that can never be effaced.

There is a story that Johnny Milne was so nervous that Rev. Kidd assisted him by adjusting the noose round Ritchie's neck and that the 'hangie' had to be pulled off the drop or else he, as well as the condemned man, would have also plunged into the void.

Poor Ritchie may not have cheated the hangman but friends were determined his body would not fall into the hands of the anatomists. He was buried at sea.

But a final word about the harrowing case of James Ritchie. Remember the Kincardineshire farmer who was reduced to penury after he turned in William Burnett, hanged for theft of a mare and an ox in 1783? Well, much the same fate overtook the person responsible for reporting Ritchie to the law. According to a contemporary writer, the man was reduced to destitution. He added, 'The popular superstition was that the blood of this unfortunate boy had cried to heaven against him.'

8

BON ACCORD GOTHIC

They called it 'Ordeal of Blood', an ancient belief that the body of a murdered person bled at the touch of the murderer. There was a hint of this macabre superstition on the eve of an Aberdeenshire farmer's funeral in the second decade of the nineteenth century, more than 200 years after King James VI, writing in *Daemonologie*, his classic guide for witch persecutors, spoke of the blood crying to heaven for revenge of the murderer.

When George Thom, a respectable sixty-one-year-old farmer and cattle-dealer, was asked to view the corpse of his youngest brother-in-law, William Mitchell, he refused. His rebuff hardened the suspicions of the mourners that Thom hid a dark secret. Previously, on the afternoon of Saturday 18 August 1821, Thom, his pock-marked face wreathed in smiles, unexpectedly turned up at the Mitchells' farm at Burnside, in the parish of Keig, near Alford. He was alone and had not visited his wife's two brothers and two sisters since their marriage less than three months earlier. Although Thom's marriage to their sister Jane (Jean) had not been popular, he was given a cordial welcome by James, William, Helen (Nelly) and Mary. James had not welcomed it but there had been no quarrel. Thom was a widower when he met Jean who, like her siblings, had never been married. The Mitchells were godly folk and well-to-do, another brother having left them a tidy sum. Jean was a wealthy woman by the time she married Thom and moved into his home at Harthill Farm, in the parish of Newhills, on the Skene turnpike, four miles from Aberdeen.

The genial Thom gave no reason for the surprise visit and agreed to spend the night. He ate some meat and later shared their supper of 'pottage' (porridge), prepared with oats, milk and salt. The sisters retired to their house at Burnside, leaving the brothers and their guest. Before they wed, Thom and his fiancée slept separately on their visits to the farm. Thom always shared a brother's room but never slept in the kitchen. That night, Thom said he would sleep in the box-bed in the kitchen but his hosts insisted he spent the night in the inner room with William. He agreed but turned down their invitation to breakfast as he had an early start and would eat at Mains of Cluny on the trek home.

James locked up before going to bed in the kitchen but awoke early next morning to hear footsteps beyond the closed wooden shutters of his box-bed. A peat fire glowed in the grate and James listened as the footfalls approached the food press. But he did not bother to investigate. When Mary and Nelly returned from milking the cows, they again asked Thom to stay for breakfast but he again turned them down. His excuse was that he wanted to clean up before people went to church. He obviously didn't want to be thought a disrespectful sinner by the churchgoers by having the dust of road on his clothes and footwear. The sisters watched Thom shake crumbs of bread and cheese, along with 'something white' on to the table. They asked what it was but he made no reply. William gave him a piece of loaf-bread and he wrapped it up in a napkin but did not put it in his pocket. Between 8 a.m. and 9 a.m. he called unannounced at Mains of Cluny where the farmer's wife, Ann Gillenders, served him tea, oatcakes, butter and an egg (but no porridge). He ate heartily and did not complain of having been unwell.

About seven miles from Aberdeen, Thom stopped a gig that was being driven towards him on the Skene turnpike by an acquaintance, Peter Farquharson, who was homeward bound to Whitehouse. Thom claimed he had travelled to Donside with the sole purpose of discussing business with Farquharson and was sorry he had not been at home when he called. No business was discussed but Thom, although he appeared healthy enough, said he had been very unwell, having eaten something that morning or the night before which had not agreed with him. He told Farquharson that, if he had not used a crow's feather to make himself throw up, he would have died. Thom had made no mention of Farquharson to the Mitchells.

Back at Burnside, Mary prepared the milk pottage in an iron pot. William ate a large helping with relish but James pushed his bowl away, complaining the porridge had a 'sweetish sickening taste'. His sisters ate without complaint. But, in no time at all, the tight-knit family would become violently ill. James felt unwell as he dressed for the walk to the kirk. His condition worsened when he was halfway there. He considered turning back but pressed on because it was Sacrament Sunday. During the service he felt himself turning blind. He staggered from the church to find William violently sick in the churchyard. James urged his brother to return with him to Burnside but William said 'people would speak if they both went home' and joined the congregation.

In between bouts of vomiting, their condition worsened. James complained of the lower part of his body 'burning within' while William, on his return from the kirk, was in agony with a 'swelling in his breast, rising to his throat'. Nelly and Mary fared no better. By the Monday, Nelly could scarcely feel the ground below her feet because of a spreading numbness from her legs downward. She had a burning pain by her heart, a 'great thirst' and a sore eyelid. Mary showed similar symptoms in her legs and had also lost the power of her left arm.

They suspected Thom of poisoning their porridge but they did not want the cause of their illness to reach the ears of their neighbours. The last thing they sought was a family scandal so they decided to remain silent. They had not even contacted their physician, Dr Murray, of Smiddyhill, Alford, in the belief they would make a complete recovery.

In the course of the next few days, William, although the worst affected, insisted on riding a mile to Whitehouse to pay his rent. He called on the doctor who prescribed a 'pitch-plaster' (a large plaster coated with a mixture of soft tar and pitch which was a favourite remedy of the times) for his chest. Dr Murray visited Burnside the following night and gave them medicine. On the Sunday, a week after Thom had left Burnside, William, who was going blind, died in the bed he shared with his brother. He rose to look for a drink and then came back to bed. He stretched himself, gave a terrible groan and then lay quiet. He was in a cold, deep sweat. James rose and hurried to his sisters. 'Wullie 'is gaun to wear awa' oot amo' (among) us,' he said.

On the night before William's funeral, George Thom and his wife invited themselves to Burnside. Their sudden appearance was an embarrassment to the family and neighbours in the house. Thom claimed he had been unwell for three days after his last visit, his body all swollen. James was told that, if the couple stayed, people would boycott the funeral, which would indicate the locals had an inkling of what Thom had done. James ordered them to leave the house, saying they had 'done ill enough there already'. They did not ask James to explain his remark. As they were about to leave, grudgingly, Nelly invited Jean to view their dead brother. Jean agreed but Thom refused.

The author of *The Black Kalendar of Aberdeen*, touching on the 'Ordeal of Blood', commented:

> We do not know whether or not there was any superstitious notion in Helen Mitchell's mind when she bade her sister look on the dead body, but in all probability there was in Thom's, when he avoided approaching it, a dread of undergoing an ordeal, of which such extraordinary relations are on record.

Nelly spoke plainly to Jean about the cause of William's death and Jean, in her turn, told Thom, 'Nelly says my brother was poisoned.' His brazen reply was that it was possible poison might have got in the burn from the toads and puddocks (frogs). But Nelly countered him, saying that the porridge had been made with milk not water.

But the game was up. On the night of 31 August, Thom and his wife were arrested in their beds by John Fyfe, a messenger at arms. Thom said he was very unwell and unable to rise. But two doctors had accompanied Fyfe from Aberdeen and decided Thom was fit enough to accompany them by carriage to the Bridewell. The vehicle stopped in Union Place, opposite the jail, and Thom completed the rest of the journey on foot although he asked Fyfe for a loan of his walking cane and moaned that the doctors did not understand what ailed him.

Jean Thom was discharged after giving a statement but George Thom stood trial for murder at the Autumn Circuit Court in Aberdeen. James Barron, a druggist in Aberdeen, told the court that on 17 August (the day before Thom appeared at Burnside) a man resembling Thom came to his shop to buy arsenic 'to poison rats'. But Barron refused to sell the poison to a complete stranger and Thom left empty-handed. The post-mortem examination revealed that 'the deceased had died by means of some deleterious matter received into the stomach'. Dr Murray, who opened the body, said the deceased showed signs of having been poisoned by sugar of lead. It was extremely improbable, he added, that an entire family would be struck down instantly by a natural disease. Four other doctors backed up his report.

In his declaration, Thom said he had gone to Aberdeen to transact business with some stablers and others, whom he named. However, they were not asked to give evidence in his defence, and nor did he produce any exculpatory evidence.

Thom remained calm and unmoved throughout the fourteen-hour-long trial even though he knew his crime had left his surviving victims so disabled it was doubtful if they would ever work again. The trial adjourned at 2 a.m. for the verdict to be delivered later. He was found guilty and sentenced to die on the gallows and his body given to the anatomists. As he was led away, he coolly brushed his hat with his hand and said to the counsel near him, 'Gentlemen, I am as innocent as any of you sitting there.'

But he had a change of mind as the day of his execution approached. He signed a document absolving his wife. He asked the Mitchells for their forgiveness and pleaded with them not to forsake Jean as 'she had no hand in what I did'. On the eve of his execution, Thom made a full confession of his diabolical crime. Envy and greed were his motives. If his attempt to commit mass murder had succeeded, his wife stood to inherit a small fortune.

Although medical evidence at his trial indicated that William Mitchell had probably died of sugar of lead poisoning, Thom confessed that he put arsenic in the salt at Burnside. Until then, it was believed that poison had been mixed with the oatmeal. The name of the person who sold him the arsenic was left blank on his public confession. Sugar of lead (lead acetate), which is used in the textile industry, is a white crystalline substance with a sweetish taste – the description of the porridge James Mitchell found so unappetising on that fateful Sabbath morning. Arsenic on the other hand has little or no taste although one leading medical authority found it to be insipid and sweetish.

Thom was tormented by malicious gossip in his final hours. One rumour swept Aberdeen that he had murdered Thomas Gill, whose body had been found in the harbour in November 1817. In his dying declaration, he emphatically denied the allegation, claiming he had been ill in bed at the time.

Thom made one last bid to cheat the hangman when his sons, daughter and nephew visited him in jail on Sunday 4 November. As he embraced one of his sons, Thom slipped a note into his hand, pleading with him to smuggle poison into the jail so he could commit suicide. But his son would have none of it and sent a letter of refusal, urging his father to submit to his punishment. The authorities were informed and the condemned man was watched round the clock by two warders.

At 2 p.m. on the day of his execution, Friday 16 November 1821, Thom, weakened by his ordeal, was brought from his cell to the court house, where he was supported while his shroud was put on and his arms pinioned by hangman Johnny Milne. In the courtroom, where the Lord Provost and the magistrates were gathered, Thom was given a chair because of his state of near collapse. Even so, he thanked them for his humane treatment in prison and, at his own request, they sang part of the 103rd Psalm, 'The Lord is merciful and gracious . . .' He remained seated as his religious advisers, Rev. Thom, no relation to the condemned man, and Rev. Kidd, who had officiated at sheep-stealer James Ritchie's execution in 1818, offered up a prayer. He was then led out to the scaffold by the two ministers. The drop fell at five minutes to three. Thom died without a struggle.

The immense crowd behaved in an orderly fashion throughout. After the body was cut down, it was conveyed in a cart, escorted by the Aberdeenshire Militia which had guarded the scaffold, to the anatomy department at Marischal College. Doctors Skene and Ewing would carry out a series of galvanic experiments to study and demonstrate the effects of electricity on the body.

It could have been a scene ripped from the pages of a Gothic horror story as the frock-coated surgeons stooped over a bloodless corpse in a gloomy anatomical chamber. A lantern glimmered on the apparatus which consisted of a heavy battery charged with a diluted solution of nitric and sulphuric acids from which dangled wires with pointed metal rods. A brief account of the 'galvanic phenomena' appeared in the press. The readers of the *Aberdeen Journal* were informed that:

> The body was brought into the dissecting room, about an hour after suspension, and still retained nearly its natural heat. The upper part of the Spinal Cord and the Sciatic Nerve were immediately laid bare, and a Galvanic Arc was then established, by applying the positive wire to the Spine, and the negative to the Sciatic Nerve, when a general convulsive starting of the body was produced.

When the apparatus was applied elsewhere, 'the hand was closed with such violence, as to resist the exertions of one of the assistants to keep it open'. A touch of a wire to certain nerves produced movement in the face muscles and the tongue. The experiment ended after an hour and a quarter when the heat of the body had diminished. Here was a terrifying echo of a controversial galvanic experiment that had been carried out by Glasgow surgeons on the corpse of a hanged criminal in 1818, the year Mary Shelley's classic tale of horror, *Frankenstein*, first appeared. Murderer Matthew Clydesdale's body was linked to a voltaic pile (a primitive electrical battery) with ghastly results for some of the spectators. The dead man's chest heaved and fell, as if he were alive, and a leg shot out with such force that a student was almost sent flying. The corpse's lifeless features twitched in apparent rage, horror, despair and anguish and it flashed ghastly grins. Clydesdale seemed to point a finger at various onlookers, some of whom fled. One man fainted. (In 1803, a beadle died of fright after a galvanic experiment was performed on a man hanged at Newgate.) There was no such disturbance from those who attended the Aberdeen experiment but it is not known how many remained to see Thom's body dissected.

George Thom was born in the parish of Alford and was a blacksmith before becoming a farmer and cattle-dealer. With such a rural background, he would probably have been aware of many of the superstitions of north-east Scotland and known of the 'Ordeal of Blood' and the old wives' tales concerning frogs and toads.

The last person to be convicted of the 'Ordeal of Blood' in Scotland was Philip Stanfield who stood trial in Edinburgh in 1688 for the murder of his father, at New Mills, East Lothian. After suspicion fell on

Philip, the body of Sir James Stanfield, a colonel with Cromwell, was exhumed at Morham churchyard in the Lammermuirs. In accordance with Scots burial custom, Philip lifted his father's head – and horrified witnesses saw blood spurting through the shroud from the neck, which Philip had touched. He had strangled the elderly man and he paid the penalty by being gruesomely executed and hung in chains at the Gallow Lee, a former place of execution near the top of Leith Walk in Edinburgh.

At Aberdour, Aberdeenshire, Brodie's Cairn took its name from a farmer who slew his mother. Everyone present was called upon to touch her naked corpse at the gate of the kirkyard but her son held back. When forced to approach the body, he confessed.

In October 1698, Jean Gordon, widow of Reverend Fraser, minister at Slains, Aberdeenshire, who had been in ill health for sometime, was found dead in bed. His stepson, also a minister, was suspected. There was no sign of violence and poison was ruled out so the 'Ordeal of Blood' was invoked. Rev. Dunbar, the minister at nearby Cruden, prayed to God that he would unmask the murderer but, when the stepson and the witnesses touched the corpse, it did not bleed.

There is also the strange case of 'Skene's Recruit', the batman of a Captain Skene, who, according to one account, was brutally murdered and whose mangled body was dumped at the Aberdeen Links. Captain Skene's regiment, which had been raised to fight in the American War of Independence, filed past his coffin in the Castlegate and, although every soldier was obliged to touch the corpse, the murderer went undetected. Fact or fiction? Curiously, the body of John Mollison, a recruit in the 73rd regiment, who had left his billet the previous evening, was found face down in a field near the foot of the Castlehill on the morning of 19 March 1778. He had been stabbed, probably with a bayonet, more than thirty times in his left side and once in the neck. His bonnet and shoes were close by but his watch and some money were missing. The *Aberdeen Journal* reported that the chief suspects, two Irish recruits, had been locked up. They were not bought to trial, however, and there was no mention of the regiment being subjected to the 'Ordeal of Blood' or whether Mollison was a batman.

9
THE VINTNERS' WIVES

Margaret Shuttleworth and Kate Humphrey had several things in common. They wed military men who became tavern keepers. Their downfall was drink and both died at the end of the Aberdeen hangman's rope for murdering their spouses. But their tragic lives, which ended nine years apart, were touched by other curious coincidences.

Attractive Peg Tindal, born of Scottish parents in Gothenburg in 1785, caught the eye of Henry Shuttleworth, a corporal in the marines, when she went to work in Sergeant Johnston's tavern opposite the well at Dummie Haa's Wynd in Montrose. Peg's widowed mother had returned from Sweden after Tindal, an innkeeper, died.

Shuttleworth, a former button-maker from Birmingham, married Margaret in Montrose and she accompanied him with his regiment to Portsmouth and later to Taunton, Somerset. He was promoted to sergeant and she enjoyed a wide circle of friends. In 1815, however, Shuttleworth was discharged from the army on half-pay and the couple returned to Montrose where he set up business as a grocer and spirits-dealer. A year later, he took over as licensee of Henry Farquharson's tavern, which fronted Castle Street, when the owner retired. Farquharson remained the Shuttleworths' landlord and near neighbour. His house was in the same close as theirs. There was access to the Shuttleworths' two-bedroomed home, which was part of the tavern, by the close which ran between Castle Street and Bridge Street. It had two gates, which were usually locked at night.

Mrs Shuttleworth drank heavily and blamed her addiction on the failure of the business. Her behaviour was so violent in front of customers that her husband feared for his and their safety and would shut up shop. The couple quarrelled incessantly and she was heard to damn him as 'a Birmingham button-making bugger'. Angry words degenerated into violence. Mrs Shuttleworth would hurl pokers and tongs at her husband. Eventually he notified Farquharson he was giving up the tavern to return to friends in England. He would leave his wife and give her an allowance of a shilling a day.

On the evening of Friday 27 April 1821, their servant, Catherine McLeod, heard the couple quarrelling. Mrs Shuttleworth, who was aware of her husband's plans to leave her, was so drunk she smashed the kitchen window with her fist. Shuttleworth complained that, in the past six months, she had cost him seven shillings for glass. The sound of breaking glass attracted Elizabeth Croll to the door of the Farquharsons' house across the close from the Shuttleworths' house. Mrs Shuttleworth was inside and her husband, who was in the close, called out to her, 'Come and see what you have done.' She replied, 'If I had the big poker I would lay your harns (brains) on the floor and let you look at that!'

McLeod was asked by her master to put his wife to bed, which she did, undressing her in Mrs Shuttleworth's bedroom, which was between the bar and the kitchen on the ground floor. Shuttleworth slept upstairs. McLeod left him sitting by the fireside drinking and went to a 'lyke-wake', the death-watch custom, to watch over the body of Henry Farquharson's niece who had died at a house on the Bridge Road.

Around 4 a.m. next morning, ex-licensee Farquharson was wakened by Mrs Shuttleworth's cry, 'Rise, Farquharson. Shuttleworth is lying in the entry and I think he is dead.' It was true. Farquharson found the bloodied body lying in the flagstoned entry passage at the foot of the stairs. From the position and appearance of the corpse, he did not think that the deceased had fallen downstairs. He had, in fact, been battered about the head with a poker. When Catherine McLeod was summoned from the 'lyke-wake' her mistress wrung her hands and cried, 'Oh, Kitty! I am past crying.' She explained she had got up for a drink in the kitchen and stumbled across the body – even though the maid had left drinking water in Mrs Shuttleworth's bedroom. Her mistress thought her husband had fallen downstairs.

Aberdeen's Castlehill Barracks looms above Hangman's Brae (left) in this 1830 drawing. Note the tavern sign above the lamp depicting a matchstick figure on the gallows. (Author's collection)

Johnny Milne, the Aberdeen 'hangie', chooses fish, one of his many perks (left), in Robert Seaton's *View of Castle Street, 1806,* which is dominated by the tolbooth steeple. (Aberdeen City Council)

The 'Hanging Stone' marks the spot where the gallows stood at the door of the Aberdeen tolbooth jail on execution days. Hence the grim jest that ne'er-do-wells would end up 'facing doon Marischal Street'. (Norman G. Adams)

The Scottish 'Maiden', the beheading machine that pre-dated the French guillotine, was used in Aberdeen.(National Museums of Scotland, Edinburgh)

Cutting edge. The blade of the Aberdeen 'Maiden' is now in the city's Museum of Civic History. (Aberdeen City Council)

The Red Kirk, Lhanbryde, where Alexander Gillan was arrested after a brutal murder in 1810. His body was left hanging in chains within sight of the church. (Author's collection)

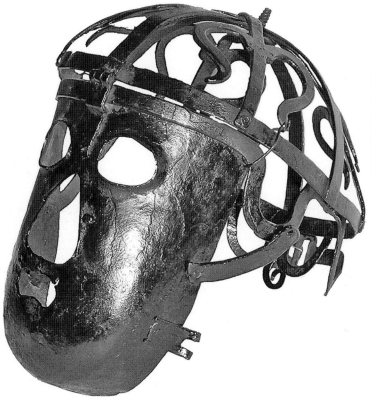

Mask of shame. This macabre version of the scold's bridle or branks, a punishment reserved for nagging wives and gossips, is displayed at Montrose Museum. (Angus Council Cultural Services)

The Warlock Stone of Craiglash Hill was the meeting place of the Deeside witches. They would suffer horribly at the stake in Aberdeen. (Ian Strachan)

Traffic fumes have replaced the stench of burning flesh in Commerce Street, Aberdeen, the site of the medieval hollow between Heading Hill (left) and Castlehill where witches were executed. (Norman G. Adams)

Tower of strength? The Aberdeen tolbooth prison, photographed from Lodge Walk, was far from escape-proof. A witty felon is supposed to have scrawled 'Rooms to Rent' on the front door after fleeing. (Aberdeen City Council)

When Peter Young, the famous caird, and his gang made a daring break-out from the Aberdeen prison in October 1787, they used brute force and guile to open these iron-bound doors. (Aberdeen City Council)

Prisoners awaiting execution in the Aberdeen tolbooth were tethered to the 'lang gade', an iron bar which restricted their mobility. (Aberdeen City Council)

Street of damnation. Kate Humphrey, the last woman to hang in Aberdeen, kept a public house in the notorious 'Bool Road', home to the 'Penny Rattler', a tawdry theatre. (Author's collection)

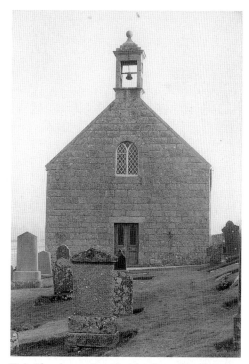

Fallen hero. Malcolm Gillespie, the Skene exciseman, proudly showed forty-two wounds to his jailers before he was hanged in Aberdeen. (Author's collection)

Tyrie Church, near Fraserburgh, where wife poisoner James Burnett and his young bride-to-be set tongues wagging in 1848. (Norman G. Adams)

The hamlet of Kirktown of St Fergus, near Peterhead, was the scene of an infamous shooting in 1853. Dr William Smith, who was cleared of murder, lived opposite the village shop. (Norman G. Adams)

The last drop. Hangman William Calcraft shook hands with John Booth, the last person to be publicly executed in Aberdeen, before he was led to the scaffold on 21 October 1857. (Alex F. Young)

Lawman George Webster, the scourge of poachers and killers in bygone Aberdeenshire, spent two nights chained to a brutal murderer. He would boast, 'That's the han' that's grippet seven murderers!' (Author's collection)

On the warpath! Peter Williamson, seen here in his Native American costume, exposed the Aberdeen white slave trade. (Robert Smith)

Peg Shuttleworth struck a fashion note when she went on trial for her life at the Circuit Court of Justiciary in Perth on 19 September 1821. The thirty-six-year-old was brought to the bar of the court wearing:

> a fashionable black bonnet and neat plain muslin cap, her hair tastefully dressed in small ringlets on each side of the forehead, a black gown and scarlet shawl, with a gold brooch at her breast; on her fingers were several rings, and she looked remarkably well.

She was allowed to remove her bonnet in the hot, stuffy courtroom. She was served soup during the proceedings. (Seven years later William Burke, of Burke and Hare infamy, and his woman, Nelly McDougal, were served bread and soup during their marathon murder trial in Edinburgh.)

Dr Henry Hoile, a local surgeon who examined Henry Shuttleworth's body, told the court he had noticed bloodstained prints of a naked foot on the stairs and in the passage above. Mrs Shuttleworth twice lied to him about going upstairs. Her hands were bloody and she was trembling. A terrier dog, which had been heard barking during the night by neighbours, lay petrified with fear in Mrs Shuttleworth's bed. A post-mortem examination revealed Shuttleworth's skull had sustained three fatal fractures. The injuries were not caused by a fall down stairs but had been inflicted by 'some ponderous, obtuse instrument' such as a poker recovered from the house. The prosecution closed its case with the reading of conflicting statements made by the accused to Montrose magistrates and the sheriff at Forfar. In the beginning, she claimed she had had 'no words' with her husband on the evening before his death but she later admitted that there had been 'high words' on the Friday afternoon but 'no particular quarrel'. Her hands had become stained with blood when she went to raise his head.

In his closing statement, Mr J. A. Maconochie, the advocate depute, said the medical evidence proved that Shuttleworth had been killed by three blows with a heavy, blunt instrument that had been wielded by his wife who was alone in the house. No one else was suspected. There was no sign of a robbery and, if her husband had been killed by someone else, the killer could not have got out again because all the doors were locked from the inside and the windows were all fastened. Mrs Shuttleworth had said she had gone to the kitchen for a drink yet there was one available in her bedroom.

Mr Robert Thomson, defending, said that, if Mrs Shuttleworth had murdered her husband, she would have had ample time in which to flee justice. Instead, she was the first to rouse her neighbours. He also reminded the jury that she was so drunk, she had to be undressed and put to bed and was, therefore, in no condition to commit the crime. Although there had been no robbery, the killer might have been disturbed by the barking of the dog.

In his address to the jury, the Lord Justice Clerk, the Right Hon. David Boyle, who sat with Lord Pitmilly, supported the medical evidence which, he said, had conclusively proved that the deceased had been the victim of violence. Mrs Shuttleworth had shown malice and ill-will towards her husband and so he recommended that they convict her of murder.

The court rose and, the following morning, the jury unanimously found the accused guilty. Sentencing her to death, the Lord Justice Clerk ordered her to be detained in Perth, on a diet of bread and water, until 1 November, when she was to be taken back to Montrose to await her execution next day. Her body was then to be delivered to the Professor of Anatomy at Edinburgh University for public dissection.

But doubts regarding the purely circumstantial evidence in the case were raised in a petition signed by 200 sympathisers and sent to King George IV. These also included: lack of real motive; her state of intoxication at the time of the crime; her guiltless behaviour in being first to raise the alarm; and that the crime had probably been committed by someone else. Mrs Shuttleworth also petitioned the monarch for clemency on the grounds that a Montrose man, whose name was never released to the public, was more likely to be the murderer. As a result, the petitioners won a four-week stay of execution. Her supporters were unable to save her from the gallows but it was unclear whether the respite had been for a calendar or lunar month. It was left to twelve English judges to rule whether or not a further extension of five days should be granted. The date of her hanging would be Friday 7 December 1821.

During the few weeks before her execution, Mrs Shuttleworth took a morbid interest in the trial of Aberdeenshire farmer George Thom, the man who had poisoned his Keig relatives. She insisted that details of his execution, as well as the 'more horrid account of the galvanic experiments upon the body previous to dissection', be read aloud to her. She disapproved of Thom's crime and said she was 'a saint in comparison to him'. Her black humour did not desert her as her dreaded day approached. In her cold, dank cell, Mrs Shuttleworth suffered from chilblains and, when a visitor suggested she get a doctor, she grimly joked that she 'need not much mind about [her] legs, as the doctors would soon have [her] body and legs together, to dress as they chose'.

Mrs Shuttleworth's ordeal on the scaffold was harrowing. After a religious service in her cell, she sipped wine before being pinioned by Aberdeen hangman Johnny Milne. Outside the prison walls, a storm demanded entry. The wind whooped in the chimney and the rain hammered on the roof. As the elements beat down on a crowd of 4,000, the majority of whom were females, the condemned woman walked to the scaffold in a steady manner, escorted by a melancholy procession made up of legal and civic figures and clergymen. Since one o'clock, the military and constables, numbering almost 400, had formed ranks in front of the jail and at the barricade around the scaffold. The funereal toll of the steeple bell heightened the sense of dread. At 2.20 p.m., Mrs Shuttleworth, dressed in black with a white apron and new black boots and black gloves, reached the gallows platform. She joined in the prayers and psalm singing but was unable to hold the psalm book by herself because of her pinioned arms and a minister assisted. She objected to the phrase 'blood guiltiness' in a verse of the 51st Psalm and it was omitted.

Milne slipped the noose about her neck but then struggled to get the white cotton nightcap over her head, it having shrunk in the rain. 'Ye're choakin' me already an' I ha'e something to say,' she complained. Her last words were, 'I die innocent – I loved my husband – I love my life – Jesus Christ have mercy on my soul.' The signal was given and Milne cut the rope supporting an upright post with an axe. The post toppled and the trapdoor opened below Mrs Shuttleworth. A man fainted at the sight. So that the assembly could get a clearer view, her body was hoisted up by the rope and a pulley which was fixed to the crossbeam. It took six minutes for her to die. Afterwards, her corpse was packed in a nondescript box and then transported incognito by road from Montrose to Pettycur in Fife. From there it was shipped across the Forth by ferry to Leith and then taken to Dr Alexander Monro's dissecting rooms in Edinburgh.

Peg Shuttleworth and Kate Humphrey, the vintner's wife from Aberdeen, were both fatalists. After Mrs Shuttleworth's execution, the first edition of her biography noted the bizarre coincidences that the date 20 September had had on her ill-omened life. She was born on 20 September 1785; a fatal accident to an infant she was nursing while watching the Montrose races occurred on 20 September 1796; she was married on 20 September 1806; and the warrant for her execution was dated 20 September 1821.

The memory of a hanging had haunted Kate Humphrey since she was a child. In 1784, Mrs Humphrey, born Catherine Davidson at Keith Hall, near Inverurie, had been taken to watch the execution of Jean Craig, a daring and habitual thief, shortly after she moved to Aberdeen. Craig, who had made three High Court appearances in two years, was condemned by Lord Gardenstone and Lord Braxfield for stealing cloth from a bleachfield at Huntly, her birthplace. She should have hanged in the marketplace in Aberdeen on 11 June but she was given a respite until 25 July. As was the custom after an execution, the executioner Robbie Welsh tossed the rope into the crowd and the frightened young Catherine was struck on the breast by the hangman's knot.

Kate was eighteen when she met and married James Humphrey, an Englishman, whose regiment, the Windsor Foresters Fencible Light Cavalry, was stationed in Aberdeen. He carried on his trade as a butcher when he left the regiment although he continued to wear the uniform of the Aberdeenshire Militia, a regiment raised from among the civil population. The first sixteen years of their married life ran smoothly although they were marred by the death of an infant, their only offspring.

Cracks appeared in their marriage when they seemed to become their own best customers in a public house they opened in Albion Street, in the east end. The street was previously known as the Bowl Road, 'Ye Boul-gat' of the records of 1593, which led eastwards from Park Road to the Links. Its name was changed in the vain hope a stroke of the pen would alter the notorious character. A tawdry theatre, known as the 'Penny Rattler', added to the area's evil reputation until it was replaced with a mission hall.

The Humphreys were in a constant state of feuding and quarrelled in front of neighbours and their servant Janet Petrie. Kate suspected her husband of infidelity and was often heard to threaten his life. During one fearful row, Humphrey tilted his throat and taunted his razor-wielding wife, saying, 'There, do it now – for you will do it sometime!' She once told a neighbour, 'Arsenic is the best thing for the scoundrel.' Humphrey made a chillingly accurate prediction that '[my] wife will hang with her face down Marischal Street for [me] yet'.

Their drunken feuds continued till the night of Friday 16 April 1830, when Kate carried out her threat. A heated row erupted after Humphrey had forcibly evicted a woman his wife had admitted into their home. The vintner harboured a suspicion that the woman, a Mrs Walton, whom he described as a 'bad character', had tried to poison her own husband and would do the same to him. Kate ordered her servant to bed before her, which was unusual. As the girl went upstairs she heard her mistress cry, 'Lord God, if anybody would give him poison and keep my hand clear of it.'

The Humphreys slept apart. Kate's room was opposite the kitchen where her husband had his bed. Humphrey was in the habit of sleeping with his mouth open and sometime during the night Kate crept into the kitchen on her stocking soles and poured a glass of vitriol (sulphuric acid) down his gaping throat. Kate woke Janet, the servant, and told her that her husband had taken ill and was making a noise. Janet reported that her mistress 'had a smile on her face as she spoke'. The girl rushed downstairs to find Humphrey writhing in agony and roaring out, 'I'm burned! I'm gone! I'm roasted!' Kate tried to calm him by assuring him he must have taken 'bad drink'. Neighbours who were drawn to the scene heard Humphrey gasp, 'Oh, woman, woman, whatever I have gotten, it was in my own house. You have tried to do this often and you have done it now.'

His bedclothes had scorch marks and a neighbour's child, who put its lips to a glass standing on the bedside table, cried out in pain. Its mother burned her fingers when she touched the glass and curious neighbours also scorched their lips on the rim. Janet Petrie spotted that there were three glasses on the table, yet, when her master retired for the night, there had only been two. A phial, kept by the kitchen window, had previously contained three or four teaspoonfuls of oil of vitriol but was now nearly empty. A small measure of vitriol added to water provided the working class with a citrus-like tonic but Kate Humphrey claimed she used the stuff to treat a wart. The alert Janet noticed that scorch marks appeared on her mistress's apron after she used it to wipe the offending glass.

A doctor could do little for the dying man. With his last breath, he absolved his wife of any crime even though, when a neighbour asked what ailed him, he replied, 'Bad work, bad work – may God Almighty forgive them who have done this to me.' On that occasion, Kate wrung her hands in despair and kissed her husband. The Rev. Mr Hugh Hart attended and, on asking if Humphrey had any suspicion of his wife, he was told, 'No, no.' He died on the Sunday, less than forty-eight hours after she had poured vitriol down his throat.

But Humphrey's dying declaration would not help his wife when she appeared at the Autumn Circuit on a charge of murdering him. Robert Christison, Professor of Medical Jurisprudence at Edinburgh University and a medical witness at the trial of the murderer William Burke in December 1828, said sulphuric acid had killed Humphrey and that two or three teaspoonfuls of the acid sold in shops would cause death. When poured down the throat of a person lying on his back, it would produce a spasm which would cause him to throw up, resulting, in this case, in the bedclothes being scorched. After a twelve-hour trial, the all-male jury returned a unanimous verdict of guilty. Lord Mackenzie showed scant sympathy to the stout, middle-aged woman at the bar as he sentenced her to death and ordered her body be given for dissection. 'You will appear before God stained with the blood of a murdered husband,' he thundered. Kate, whose composure had impressed the court during the proceedings, finally collapsed in tears. 'Oh, no, my lord,' she sobbed, 'I didna do't – oh, no, no!'

The *Aberdeen Chronicle* reporter no doubt tingled his readers' spines with this description of the dark deed:

> As her unconscious victim lay buried in sleep, with open mouth on the bed, which she had shared with him for 33 years, she appeared softly near the midnight hour with the instrument of death in her hand, and, steeled to the feelings of pity and remorse, administered the fatal draught which was to burn up the sources of life.

On the day after her trial, Kate confessed her guilt, saying that she had been driven by jealously and malice excited by the misconduct of her husband and dislike he bore towards her. On the eve of her execution, Kate had barely twenty minutes' sleep because of the hammering by carpenters as they built her gallows in Castle Street. Mrs Shuttleworth was also disturbed in her sleep by violent strokes on the gibbet but hooligans rather than carpenters were to blame. (The noise of workmen building murderer William Allan's gallows at the door of Aberdeen tolbooth on his final night 'seemed to shake his very soul'. On the day of his execution, 10 February 1826, he fainted three times while being led to the scaffold – the last time on the drop itself.)

'O, it's a sair thing to wash for the gibbet; but I hope I will be washed in the blood of my Redeemer', groaned Kate, as she prepared for the scaffold. At 2.30 p.m. on Friday 8 October 1830, Kate Humphrey (51), 'genteelly dressed in black', was led from the nearby East Jail on the arms of her jailers. The first stop was the old courthouse where the Lord Provost and magistrates were gathered. The 51st Psalm, part of which Mrs Shuttleworth had objected to, was sung. Drink, Kate told them, was her downfall. But did they heed her warning as they gathered in the nearby Lemon Tree Tavern for a post-execution dram? In a clear, firm voice she went on, 'Gentlemen, you who have it in your power should look to the public houses in the quarter where I lived, for many of them are in a bad state and have much need to be looked after.'

Expressing a desire that the world would take warning by her case, Rev. Kidd, who had prayed with Kate in her cell, endorsed what she had said, adding, 'That if such houses were not put down there would be a dissolution of society.' (This warning appears to have gone unheeded for seven years later Aberdeen, with a population of just 60,000, had 870 premises where drink could be bought. There was one public house for every eleven families in the parish of Greyfriars.) Kate was close to fainting as she was positioned on the drop by hangman John Scott, the assistant hangman in Edinburgh who would later become the Aberdeen executioner. She never once lifted her eyes to look around at the huge crowd that pressed around the scaffold and stretched back as far as St Catherine's Wynd in Union Street. She dropped a napkin as a signal to Scott, who 'proceeded to do his duty'. Her last words were, 'Oh, my God . . .'

At five minutes to three, the drop fell. It had taken at least half an hour from the time she had left her cell to the moment she was hanged. The British executioner Albert Pierrepont told a Royal Commission into hanging in 1949 that, in his experience, the average time that elapsed between entering a cell and the drop was between nine and twelve seconds.

But Kate's ordeal had not ended. She struggled at the end of the rope and twice raised her hands as if praying. The crowd grew restless but they eventually slipped away, under the gaze of the ranks of special constables. Her corpse hung for forty minutes before it was cut down and taken round the corner to Marischal College where Dr Pirrie waited patiently with a group of medical students and a handful of private professional people. Kate Humphrey was the first woman to be executed in Aberdeen since Elspet Reid on 14 January 1785. Reid should have been hanged on the market-place gallows with Kate's nemesis, Jean Craig, but was respited due to pregnancy. Kate was also the last woman to be executed in the Aberdeen while Mrs Shuttleworth was the first – and last – woman to perish on the gallows in Montrose.

In 1816, a Banffshire vintner's wife Helen Reid, a mother of five, was sentenced to hang for the murder of her husband, who was also a mail contractor in Keith. The couple had been married for twenty years but her husband's business was failing. His hot temper and her addiction to drink proved a fatal cocktail and consequently, on 7 September 1815, she stabbed him in the back with a table knife. After an eight-hour trial at the Spring Circuit in Aberdeen the following year, Lord Pitmilly sentenced her to hang on 31 May and ordered her body be given to the anatomists. She was supported from the court by two officers such was the poor woman's shock. Twenty days before her scheduled execution, Helen, who was confined to the tolbooth on bread and water, was told the Prince Regent had granted a reprieve. The death sentence was later commuted and she was banished overseas for life.

10

FALLEN HERO

The De'il's awa' wi' the Exciseman

Robert Burns (1759–96)

On a moonlit moor near Midmar Lodge in Aberdeenshire, a bull terrier pioneered today's police dog work when its master turned it loose on a gang of whisky smugglers. The historic encounter took place on 8 February 1816 when the terrier became a fighting fury as it scattered the Highlanders and their packhorses laden with casks of illicit Scotch. The dog was trained to seize a horse by the nose, forcing the terrified beast to shed its load. History has not left us the name of the remarkable dog but its owner was the fearless Malcolm Gillespie, who, next to Burns, was probably Scotland's most famous exciseman. His life, however, ended in infamy.

Gillespie, who came from Dunblane, began his working life as a soldier at the age of seventeen. For three years, he served as a recruiting officer at Brechin with the First Regiment of Foot. In that time, he recruited '400 fine young lads' to the colours and seemed destined for a commission with the Prince of Wales Fencibles. But, in 1799, the twenty-year-old Gillespie, now married with a young family, entered the excise service in East Lothian. His job was to watch over and superintend the salt manufacturers at Prestonpans and he was soon adept at uncovering fraud by unfair traders in the industry.

After two years, he was transferred to the Aberdeen area at his own request. His first posting was Collieston where upwards of 1,000 casks of foreign spirits were being landed every month. The parish had been a hotbed of smuggling for many years and the grave of Philip Kennedy, killed in a clash with excisemen in 1798, survives at nearby Slains kirkyard. The zealous Gillespie, often working round the clock, was the terror of the Collieston smugglers and, by the time he left, illegal trade had been wiped out in that part of the Buchan coast. In the six years he was stationed there, he seized over 10,000 gallons of foreign spirits, fifteen horses and as many carts and destroyed 1,000 gallons. In 1807, Gillespie was appointed to Stonehaven and, thanks to his inside information, revenue cutters successfully pursued foreign luggers involved in coastal smuggling. Along the Kincardineshire coastline, smuggling was being virtually eradicated and Gillespie's reputation as a fearless and zealous opponent of law-breakers was assured.

In 1812, Gillespie was posted at his own request to the notorious Skene 'Ride', or district, a wild and desolate stretch of Aberdeenshire between the Dee and Don and a well-trodden route to Aberdeen for Highland whisky smugglers.

The gauger, as an exciseman was known, was now in his element as he found himself at the centre of several running battles with smugglers from which he escaped death on several occasions. His first bloody encounter took place one night in August 1814 when he surprised four 'notorious and determined delinquents' with a horse-drawn cart containing eighty gallons, two miles from Skene. He withstood a brutal beating and was determined to make a seizure. He shot and wounded the smugglers' horse to prevent them from getting away. The gunshot attracted the attention of some people and the smugglers were arrested.

In a pitched battle with some old foes, the Grants, at the Hill of Auchronie, near Kinellar, in August 1815, his horse lost an eye and he was injured by well-aimed stones. In 1816, Gillespie decided to enlist the help of a dog. He bought a bull terrier at considerable expense from a character as colourful as himself, Captain Robert Barclay Allardice of Ury, a keep-fit fanatic and patron of boxing who trained the bare-knuckle fighters John Gully and Tom Cribb at his estate on the outskirts of Stonehaven. Captain Barclay (he preferred to drop his additional surname) was the toast of the Fancy, the name given to the men who religiously followed sport in Regency times. He was no mean athlete. At the age of twenty, he lifted an eighteen-stone man from the floor to a table with one hand. In 1809, Barclay's most legendary exploit was winning a 1,000 guinea-wager by walking 1,000 miles in 1,000 successive hours at Newmarket – and in a top-hat, too!

Gillespie prized the dog highly. He told an acquaintance that he valued the dog above everything and 'would not have disposed of it for 100 guineas'. Unfortunately, the dog's career was short-lived. After putting smugglers to flight at Midmar Lodge and Cottown of Kintore, it was killed by a random shot during a skirmish at Parkhill on the banks of the Don on 1 August 1816.

On the night of 30 December 1818, near Kintore, Gillespie had a close call of his own when he and two assistants ambushed a gang of smugglers who were making for Aberdeen with eight horses laden with whisky. But, as Gillespie leapt from his hiding place with a sabre in one hand and a pistol in the other, he was confronted in the darkness by a dozen Highlanders. In the bloody encounter that followed, the gauger of Skene had his chin laid open by a sabre. In retaliation, he shot and wounded two gang members and the rest were driven off. Gillespie continued to live dangerously. In his last major clash near Inverurie, in January 1824, he described how 'bloody heads, hats rolling on the road, the reports of alternate firing and other noise resembled more the battle of Waterloo than the interception of a band of lawless desperadoes'. Gillespie captured 410 gallons of whisky, fourteen horses and ten carts. Eighty gallons of whisky could not be saved. Gillespie, writing in his memoirs, commented it was fortunate no lives were lost although he would probably 'carry some of the wounds [he] then received with [him] to the grave'. Prophetic words, indeed. His tally of seizures during his career totalled an imposing: 14,391 gallons of foreign spirits; 6,535 gallons of whisky, which was either impounded or destroyed; 165 horses and 85 carts; 62,400 gallons of wash (fermenting malt); and 407 stills which were destroyed.

But an excise officer was grossly underpaid and relied heavily on the proceeds of seizures for a decent living. The Treasury and the officer shared these proceeds equally but various legal fees and other expenses were the officer's responsibility. Gillespie estimated that a seizure cost him £1 per cask and he was inevitably out of pocket. He also had to pay informants and staff while the expense of running Crombie Cottage, his home at Skene, was considerable. The cottage was on a thirty-eight-year lease and he had spent £1,000 on improvements.

In July 1826, Gillespie, who by now was deeply in debt, received information that the Board of Excise planned to transfer him to another district far from the Skene Ride. The move was put on hold after some influential friends, including Captain Barclay of Ury, Provost Gavin Hadden of Aberdeen (he and eldest brother James each held office for four terms) and several distillery owners, petitioned his employers to keep him at Skene. To add weight to their argument Gillespie sent the Board a memoir of his life, virtually an autobiography, and details of his seizures. But Gillespie, facing bankruptcy and disgrace, took a desperate gamble as his debts continued to grow.

With the help of his confidential clerk, Skene Edwards, Gillespie conspired to forge bills of credit to solve his financial affairs. Edwards was not above such trickery as both he and his brother, John, who also worked at Crombie Cottage, had criminal records. Indeed, it later became clear that the gauger and members of his gang were bigger rogues than the smugglers.

A wealthy farmer, Alex Smith, of Blackhills, Skene, was unwittingly responsible for Gillespie's downfall. He was a long-time friend of the gauger and promised to help him. Smith wrote to the manager of his Aberdeen bank, the Town and County, and asked him to discount any 'bills of accommodation' bearing his endorsement which Gillespie might present. But Smith's name was not the only one on these bills. They also bore the signatures of various local farmers who apparently agreed to settle the amount due promptly or in advance. The manager did as he was told as Smith, who was in his nineties, was a valued customer. By early 1827, no fewer than twenty-two bills, valued at £554 10s, passed across the manager's desk and the money was collected by Gillespie (as drawer he was the true debtor while an acceptor acted as guarantor). But the manager and farmer Smith were unaware that the signatures of the other 'acceptors' were forgeries.

Skene Edwards had forged the names on blank bills by copying them on a windowpane over the genuine signatures, when he was able to get them. John Pratt, the miller at Mill of Ord, had signed passes for malt so Gillespie possessed his signature. Some of the names were fictitious and, in one case, the farmer was dead and buried.

Before the fraud was revealed, Gillespie had sunk to new depths. He decided to recoup his ruined fortune by torching Crombie Cottage and claiming the insurance money. He insured his thatched property for £530 with the Palladium Life and Fire Assurance Society of London and £300 with the Phoenix Assurance Society. Sometime before the blaze, a quantity of gunpowder and bottles of turpentine were stored in the barn and rope and rosin were put in the cellar.

The date set for the crime was the night of 21 February 1827, when Gillespie was attending a trial in Edinburgh. Two of his daughters were at home but took no part in what happened. Before leaving for the capital Gillespie called together his housekeeper Jessy Greig, Skene and John Edwards and a servant William Jenkins. The sly Gillespie did not speak plainly of his intentions but told them there would be 'no harm' in burning the house as it would 'take him out of his present difficulties'.

On the previous day, John Edwards and another servant George Brownie packed kindling between the joists of the house and smeared melted rosin on the furniture. Edwards then sprinkled turpentine and gunpowder through the house but spared the west room. Brownie trimmed the roof thatch between the west room and the rest of the cottage in order to save the room.

The Edwardses left about 7 p.m. and Jenkins went to his bed in the stable loft after his accomplices promised to waken him when 'the thing should be set a-going'. When Jenkins returned from the loft, Jessy Greig, who was the head of the household with Gillespie away, gave each person present a dram. Brownie lit two candles and gave one to Lexy Campbell, a loyal servant of thirteen years' service who was Gillespie's mistress. She went down into the cellar while Brownie went into the next room to set fire to the rope. The house was soon full of smoke. It was about midnight. Brownie retired and gave instructions to let him be in bed before they raised the alarm.

Crombie Cottage, west wing and all, was burned to the ground. On his return a satisfied Gillespie did not ask how the blaze had broken out but commented the thing had been 'genteelly done'. But Gillespie's world was about to collapse. So far, he had met his obligations regarding payment of the accommodation bills before they became due. In his correspondence with the Town and County and other Aberdeen banks, Gillespie had asked that correspondence regarding the bills should be sent directly to him and not the acceptors. The banks had agreed. But one of the bill-notices demanding payment was not posted to Gillespie. It was addressed to Joseph Low, Bogfairley, Newhills, one of the so-called acceptors. But Low, a humble crofter, could not read nor write. Three years earlier, Gillespie had made a seizure of whisky at his croft. Now he returned with Brownie to claim Low had signed the accommodation bill but he had been too drunk to remember. Gillespie urged the crofter to take the bill and pleaded, 'It will save me from the rope.' But it was too late. Low had already been in Aberdeen to report the affair to the procurator fiscal.

Gillespie made a final appeal to his benefactor, Smith of Blackhills, but, on being rebuffed by the farmer's young wife, Agnes Ramsay, who threatened to report him to the bank, he replied, 'For God's sake, my good madam! Don't do that. If the Fiscal was to get notice of it, I might as well cut myself to pieces!'

On 30 April 1827, the gauger was arrested while asleep in a bothy near Crombie Cottage. When John Fyfe, the Aberdeen messenger at arms who detained George Thom the poisoner in 1821, showed him his warrant Gillespie said, 'Good God! I'm a gone man. You must let me disappear until this matter be settled.' Fyfe's assistant rounded up a drunken Skene Edwards and they were taken to the Aberdeen tolbooth.

At the Circuit Court of Justiciary in Aberdeen in September, Gillespie and Skene Edwards denied charges of forgery and uttering – the act of putting forged or counterfeit coins, banknotes or promissory notes into circulation. Advocate Depute Archibald Alison confined his proof to seven of the original twenty-two charges. During the fifteen-hour-long trial, Gillespie's counsel, along with witnesses Brownie, Greig and Campbell, who were in custody, tried to fix the entire blame upon Skene Edwards. Edwards had written the body of the bills but they were all uttered by Gillespie.

After the mammoth sitting, the jury retired. It was now 1.30 a.m. on Saturday the 29th and, although the jurors had already reached their verdict, they were instructed to return at half past ten to deliver it. When the appointed hour arrived, one juror, James Davidson, was missing and it was four hours before he was fetched from his home at Kinmundy. In answer to a reprimand from the bench, Davidson said he thought his duty had ended when the verdict was 'sealed'. The jury foreman handed the judges an envelope with an ominous black seal. Gillespie was found guilty of seven charges of forgery and uttering and sentenced to death. Even if he had been acquitted, he would have still faced the charges of fire-raising with intent to defraud.

The judges, Lords Pitmilly and Alloway, referred to Gillespie's altered circumstances. Lord Pitmilly, addressing the judge at his side, said:

> My Lord Alloway, the duty which it now remains for us to discharge towards the prisoner at the bar is at all times a distressing duty; but I must say that I perform it in the present instance with feelings more than usually painful. I do not at this moment forget the various occasions on which I have seen that unhappy man in this court in a very different situation from that in which he is now placed, and that on these occasions I have had to express my approbation of his zeal and activity as an Officer of Revenue. The recollection of these things has not been absent from my mind a single moment since this trial commenced, and I could scarcely make myself believe that so sad a reverse has taken place.

Lord Alloway, before pronouncing doom, told Gillespie that he was a man possessed of talents, which might have raised him to an eminent place amongst his contemporaries, but added, 'Your fate will be a warning to the present generation. Your case will show them that persons must not trust to talents, however great, to save them from conviction. Sooner or later punishment will overtake the guilty.'

Edwards was found guilty of forgery but, after objections by his counsel, the case was passed to the High Court in Edinburgh for an opinion. He was eventually transported for seven years.

Lexy Campbell and George Brownie were then placed at the bar on charges of wilful fire-raising at Crombie Cottage and intent to defraud the insurance companies. They denied the charges but later changed their pleas to guilty of fire-raising but not guilty to fraud. This was accepted by the advocate depute. They were each sentenced to seven years' transportation. If they had been convicted of the original charges, they would have been hanged.

Gillespie, who was fifty, was a figure of hate in the Highlands and it was rumoured that a band of smugglers, wearing tartan and headed by a piper, would attend his execution in the Castlegate on Friday 16 November 1827. It proved a false rumour. Gillespie pinned his hopes on a reprieve but his fate was sealed even though he protested his innocence to the end. In the death cell, he wrote his dying declaration which was no more than a rant against Skene and John Edwards, Jenkins and Brownie whom he accused of looting and burning Crombie Cottage. The battling gauger showed jailers the forty-two wounds inflicted on various parts of his body during his life and an artist sketched his likeness for his published autobiography. The portrait which shows a sabre scar on his face is signed, 'I am Sir your unfortunate M. Gillespie'.

On the eve of his execution, he took leave of his family. He slept peacefully enough for a condemned man. In the old courthouse, a few steps from the scaffold, Gillespie sipped a tumbler of water as he addressed the magistrates. His protested his innocence to the end and walked on to the gallows platform with a firm and steady step.

The huge crowd fell silent as he took his place on the drop. There was a brief touching moment when he fixed his gaze westwards in the direction of Skene with a 'peculiarly melancholy expression'. The more cynical might believe he avoided the final ignominy of 'facing doon Marischal Street'. He gave the signal to the hangman and died with 'little if any struggle'.

After Gillespie's body was cut down, it was taken by friends for burial in Skene kirkyard. At the beginning of the last century, it was said a curious sexton exhumed the coffin and found it contained only stones. Gillespie's corpse may have been snatched by grave robbers. If the deed was the work of bodysnatchers, his body was stolen before burial. Why else fill the coffin with stones to give the impression a body was inside?

A fantastic solution to the mystery might be that Gillespie had somehow 'cheated the widdie' and was still breathing when cut down!

11
BAD TASTE

Tongues clicked like knitting needles in the Buchan parish of Tyrie when folk heard that James Burnett, who buried his invalid wife the day after her death, planned to wed a servant lass who was much younger than he was. The banns of marriage between Burnett (45) and twenty-four-year-old Jane Carty were proclaimed at the tiny parish church of St Andrews and a date fixed for the wedding ceremony. But, when the gossip reached the ears of the law, Burnett's fate was sealed and there would be no marriage.

Burnett, a farm servant, was described as a kind and attentive husband to his wife, Margaret, a mother of four sons and four daughters, who for the past five years had walked with a crutch after a stroke had left her paralysed down her left side. But, after almost quarter a century of marriage, they lived virtually separate lives. Mrs Burnett shared her small croft at Skelmanae with her daughter Margaret and young son, Thomas, the rest of the family having left home. Her husband, a stout, powerful man with long bushy hair, lived and worked at the farm of Protshaugh, no great distance across the fields from his housebound spouse. Her estranged husband shared his bed at Protshaugh with Jane Carty. She had refused to run away with him but did agree to marry him should he become a widower. Little did she imagine the demons that tormented her lover.

On the night of Wednesday 1 November 1848, Burnett visited his sick wife after feeding the horses at Protshaugh. Mr W. S. Wood, the New Pitsligo druggist, had given him some purgative powders to 'rid the stuff away from her stomach'. Although Mrs Burnett had expressed no desire for the medicine as she felt much better, he made her drink it – mixing the powder with jelly and sugar in a tea cup, which he later broke. Margaret was in the kitchen, which was where her mother slept, and saw her mother drink the medicine. The girl was ordered to bed by her father who said he would spend that night at Skelmanae. But she heard her mother being violently sick and, when she re-entered the kitchen, she saw her father, who was fully dressed, standing with his back to the peat fire and staring at his wife.

Mrs Burnett's condition worsened and, when Burnett went to comfort her, she told him, 'Hand awa'. She also refused his offer of water. He then asked if he should fetch 'that cratur', meaning the druggist, Wood, but the dying woman said she was done with doctors and cried out, 'I am poisoned! I am poisoned! God reward them upon earth for what they've done to me!' (It was an echo here of Kate Humphrey's husband's dying words.) Burnett did not appear concerned about his wife's plight and, although Strichen and New Pitsligo were only a few miles away and there was a good horse in their married son's stable close by, he did not fetch medical help.

At 5 a.m. on the Thursday, Burnett's daughter-in-law, Christian, who was married to the son with the horse, was roused from her bed by her father-in-law. He told her, 'The auld wife's a' wrang – haste ye rise!' Christian hurried to the croft where she found Mrs Burnett in agony. She had lost her hearing and died an hour later. Earlier that morning, while Christian and Margaret nursed Mrs Burnett, Burnett showed them the packets of purgative powder he had got from the druggist.

But when Burnett called at the house the previous night he also had a three-penny dose of arsenic in his pocket.

There was little or no time for mourning. At breakfast Burnett made arrangements to have the deceased buried at Strichen churchyard on the very next day, Friday 3 November, between noon and one. An old woman, Janet Robertson, a neighbour, who assisted in laying out the corpse, 'saw nae sign o' his being grieved'. It was uncommon to bury the dead so quickly, except in cases where they had succumbed to an infectious disease. Janet, however, was of the opinion that the body was not in such a state of decay that it required a hasty burial.

In mid December, rural policemen James Forsyth and Peter Sharp appeared on Burnett's doorstep at Protshaugh and asked some awkward questions about his wife's death. (Charles Lowe, of Memsie, told me that his great-grandfather John Lowe, a stonemason, was rudely awakened by the policemen and ordered to indicate the flickering lights of Protshaugh. John would not be rushed, insisting he was warmly wrapped up before facing the cold night air!)

Forsyth and his colleague had gone to Protshaugh as a result of the rumours he had heard concerning Burnett and his wife's death. When questioned about the powder she had taken, Burnett lied by saying she could not do without it. Constable Forsyth advised him to get her body exhumed but Burnett said he could not bear the idea of seeing that done. The policeman told him he did not need to be present at the exhumation and Burnett made the excuse he could not afford the expense. Forsyth countered by telling him, 'If you will allow me to say you want it done, perhaps the fiscal may do it at the public expense.' The reply was, 'Oh, I don't think it. I don't know well what to bid you say.' Next day, Forsyth reported his findings to the procurator fiscal. A check of druggists in Strichen, New Pitsligo and Boyndlie revealed that no arsenic had been sold for many months. At New Pitsligo, Mr Wood, confirmed that the purgatives he sold to Burnett were not dangerous. His helper, Christian Shand, who was present, remembered Burnett telling them his wife was very ill – and not expected to live long.

Twenty-five mourners had attended Mrs Burnett's funeral at Strichen. But, when grave-digger George Simpson opened her grave on 12 December, there was only a handful of witnesses. The coffin was laid out in the aisle of the parish church. After Margaret and Christian Burnett had identified the body, a post-mortem examination was carried out there and then by Dr Gavin, of Strichen, and a Dr Robb, in the presence of the procurator fiscal. The signs were that death was due to arsenic poisoning. The victim's organs were sealed in bottles and sent to Edinburgh where an analyst found traces of pure arsenic – more than enough to account for the death. Four days after the exhumation, Burnett was arrested at Protshaugh. He told the arresting officer, 'God help me.'

When Burnett appeared at the Spring Circuit Court of Justiciary in Aberdeen on 25 April 1849, he answered the charge of murder with a feeble, 'not guilty'. A vital witness, Elizabeth McDonald, who ran a postal delivery service between Tyrie and Fraserburgh, was approached by Burnett the Friday before his wife died to go some errands for him. He gave her half-a-crown for a New Testament and writing paper. He hesitated over his next request for arsenic. 'He did not know if it was fair (straightforward) or not,' said the witness. 'I said if it was fair he would have it.'

Burnett's excuse for wanting the arsenic was that his 'chaumer' (sleeping quarters for farm servants in Banff and Buchan) was plagued by 'rottans' (rats). After receiving an assurance he would take great care where he placed the poison, McDonald agreed to buy a small quantity for him. The following day, she left George Macdonald's chemist shop in Fraserburgh with three small wrappers each bearing the warning, 'Arsenic. Poison'. Before the transaction could be completed, she left her name and that of the accused.

On the day before Mrs Burnett died, Burnett inquired if McDonald had any mail for him. In conversation, he mentioned that his wife was 'a' failed now' but, even so, he placed an order for a bottle of wine for her. When leaving McDonald, he mentioned he was 'getting rest now' – meaning, as she understood it, that he was no longer annoyed with the rats.

It was to be expected that there would be rats around the farm but Burnett's workmates had either seen no rats, dead or alive, in the chaumer or had not been bothered by rats as often as he had claimed. The tenant farmer, Mr Pittendrigh found Burnett an excellent character but had refused his request for arsenic to destroy the vermin.

Burnett's bride-to-be Jane Carty slept in the kitchen with another servant but frequently visited the chaumer where Burnett and an eleven-year-old boy stayed. She showed considerable reluctance when Mr Deas, for the prosecution, asked her, 'Was it agreed between you and him before his wife's death that you should be married to him when she died?' The witness hesitated to answer and the question was repeated. After another long pause, she replied, 'Yes. He said that, if she did not get well now, she would not be long to the fore.' She agreed that, when his wife was alive, he had asked her to leave the country with him but she had turned him down. After Mrs Burnett's death, their banns were proclaimed at the parish kirk and the wedding day set.

The defence counsel, Mr Miller, also questioned Jane about her relationship with the accused. 'Were you on terms of intimacy with

Burnett before his wife's death?' he asked. 'Yes,' she replied. 'Was the room in which you slept near that in which the prisoner slept?' 'It was not terrible far frae it,' responded Carty.

Mr Miller asked if there was any time when she left her own room to go into Burnett's. 'I had no errand there,' she replied after a pause. Miller retorted, 'I am not asking whether you had any errand, I am asking whether you left your own room at night and went into the room where Burnett slept?' After a minute's silence, she replied softly, 'Yes.' She then admitted sharing his bed on occasional nights. Miller no doubt hoped to prove that the Protshaugh Jezebel had bewitched his client into getting rid of his ailing wife by murder even though she was innocent of his wicked scheme.

One of the judges, Lord Mackenzie, was in no doubt of the reason for the murder. In his charge to the fifteen-man jury, he said:

> I fear that there is the appearance of a very gross motive – a motive which has operated to produce murderous actions in many cases. The motive proved in evidence is that this unfortunate man, although he had a wife and family, had abandoned himself to the embraces of an adulteress. He had to do with a younger woman, a girl in the house where he resided, and he had entered into an engagement with her, which was to be completed on the death of his wife.

For most of the trial Burnett sat with his head in his hands. During a recess he was allowed to leave the dock for a glass of water. He asked a court officer how he viewed the case. 'It looks very black,' he was told. 'Which are the blackest points?' he inquired. 'Oh, that's hard to say – it is all black alike,' was the honest response.

The jury saw it that way, too. After a mere five minutes, they returned with a unanimous verdict of guilty. Lord Moncrieff, proposing sentence of death, agreed with their verdict. It was left to Lord Mackenzie to don the black cap, warning Burnett there was no hope of a pardon. The prisoner received his fate with his head deeply buried in his hands but, as he led away, he wailed, 'I am innocent – I am innocent.'

The date of his execution was Tuesday 22 May 1849. On the appointed day, Burnett slept for three hours during the night and was joined in prayers at five in the morning by Rev. Mr W. D. Strahan, the chaplain of the East Jail, who found him in a 'very satisfactory state of mind'. At six, the prisoner managed to breakfast on bread and tea. Rev. Dr Mackintosh then engaged Burnett in 'devotional exercise'.

A reporter from the *Aberdeen Herald* set the grim scene in Castle Street:

> The scaffold was erected at an early hour on Tuesday morning and (though there was little 'clank' of carpenters' hammers, as the whole apparatus is fastened with screws) the glare of the flaring artificial lights, the steelness of the morning, and the gloomy appearance of the fatal apparatus, are described by those who witnessed the scene as having a peculiarly striking and ghastly effect.

In his cell Burnett and the ministers sang 'The Hour of my Departure's Come' and, shortly after eight, the hangman appeared and pinioned his arms. As the procession, led by Mr Chalmers, the prison governor, moved through a passage to the old burgh court, the condemned man shut his eyes so as not to be unnerved by the crowd. They were still tightly shut when the procession halted before a group of magistrates and the Lord Provost, who asked Burnett three questions: 'Do you adhere to your confession of the crime for which you are to suffer?' – 'Yes.'; 'Are you satisfied with the attention shown to you in jail?' – 'Perfectly so, in every respect.'; and, finally, 'Have you any statement to make to the Magistrates?' At this point, Rev. Strahan read the prisoner's dying confession:

> I have confessed my sin that I am to suffer for, to man, and I hope God will forgive me for all my sins for Christ's sake; and in your presence, gentlemen, I declare there was no one knew of it but myself. I confessed all to Mr Strahan, the chaplain. May God be merciful to me, a sinner, for Christ's sake. Amen.

In a letter to the prison governor, Burnett admitted hatching his murderous plan ten days before he carried it out and, from that time, he said 'the most fearful dreams haunted [his] pillow and banished sleep'. Jane Carty also received a letter in which he asked for her forgiveness. A crowd of about 12,000 – 'almost all', according to the *Herald*, 'without exception, from the lower class of our population' – was prevented from reaching the foot of the scaffold by ranks of special constables. There were no unruly scenes although the hangman was 'assailed with repeated yells of execration'. He was probably John Murdoch, a former Glasgow baker, who was eighty-four when he performed his last hanging in Glasgow two years later. He was Britain's oldest ever hangman and he tottered to the gallows with the aid of a walking stick.

The *Herald*'s rival, the *Aberdeen Journal*, commented on the turnout at the first execution since Kate Humphrey's in 1830, saying, 'The crowd was immense – considering that the factories were purposely kept at work – and formed one dense mass from near the Cross to the head of the Shiprow.' (Earlier in the century, Miss Betsy Gray, who ran a private school in Stronach's Close in Castle Street, confined her pupils to the classroom for seven hours on the day of an execution to spare their 'young feelings'.)

Burnett's last words were, 'Lord have mercy on my soul.' Death was instantaneous. His body was cut down after less than an hour but, as bodies of executed murderers were no longer to be made available for dissection, he was buried within the precincts of the prison. In the next eight years, it would be joined by the corpses of three more executed murderers.

William Skene, author of *East Neuk Chronicles*, ventured as far as the Duke of Gordon's statue in the Castlegate on the day they hanged Burnett. His youthful gaze took in the terrible pageant. He wrote:

> The procession made its appearance through a window in the Town House. The town's officers, to the number of eight or ten, headed by Charlie Dawson, Horne, Mellis and Leslie, led the van, and then followed the culprit, supported by warders and prison officials. The wretched man wore a black suit and a white nightcap, and he was attended by Rev. Dr Macintosh, of the East Church. As soon as the procession appeared, I fled the scene, and saw no more of James Burnett.

Aberdeen juries showed shameless timidity in convicting the accused in two other murder trials where poison was administered. At the Circuit Court, before Lord Eskgrove in April 1795, Anne Inglis, a servant, was indicted for the murder of her master and lover Patrick

Pirie, of Malhereust, in the parish of Alvah, Banffshire. The woman believed the thirty-two-year-old bachelor planned to marry her but, when he chose another, Inglis was heard to say that 'there would be a burial before a bridal'. Shortly before his wedding, Pirie was seized with violent stomach pains and vomiting but, having a strong constitution, he recovered. But, a fortnight later, he collapsed with worse symptoms after being served ale by Inglis. He lingered for nine days and, before he died, accused her.

A post-mortem disclosed 'much inflammation in the stomach, the inner coat of which was corroded, and separated from the adjoining one'. There was no trace of arsenic but the surgeons suspected the victim had swallowed blue vitriol (copper sulphate). A search of a chest belonging to Inglis turned up a paper parcel containing the poison. The accused claimed it was for the toothache but that was a lie. After a trial lasting thirteen hours, she was found not guilty.

The Autumn Circuit Court of 1827 had handed out a death sentence to the crooked exciseman Malcolm Gillespie. But handsome John Lovie (40), who farmed Futteretden at Mains of Fingask, near Fraserburgh, was spared when he was tried at the same sitting for murdering servant Margaret Mackessar. Margaret, or Meggie as she was known, was expecting his baby and she had told her sister that they were getting married. Lovie took an unhealthy interest in different poisons and asked a farmhand if he knew which would cause an abortion. On visits to Fraserburgh, he bought the purgative drug, jalap, and arsenic – to get rid of rats, he claimed. On 14 August, 'Meggie' took violently ill after eating breakfast. As her condition worsened, Lovie, who was ploughing, remarked that if she did not get better she would not be 'lang to the fore'. He kept her family in the dark about her illness and did not even fetch her mother or a doctor till it was too late.

Two days after the funeral, the body, despite Lovie's objections, was lifted and doctors removed the internal organs and sent them to Edinburgh for expert analysis. Lovie asked one of the witnesses of the exhumation if 'the body would swell if the girl had been poisoned'. The surgeons disclosed that Margaret had been six-months pregnant and the cause of death was arsenic poisoning. Before his arrest, a friend advised Lovie to fly the country. The deceased's sister, Jean, said Lovie told her that he 'would rather put a knife to his own heart, than to have harmed her'. In his declaration, Lovie denied his affair with the deceased and said he had no idea she was pregnant. He did not know that the substance he bought from the druggist was poisonous and had used the stuff to kill vermin on the backs of his cattle. His statements at the trial were proved false and the defence called no witnesses. It was left to the future Lord Cockburn, Lovie's counsel, to sow the seeds of doubt in the minds of the jury and, after deliberating for only half an hour, the verdict was not proven.

12
SLAUGHTER AT KITTYBREWSTER

'Airt and pairt in Downie's slaughter' is an obsolete Aberdeen proverb that can be traced to a dubious story of ritual murder. Downie or Dauney, legend tells us, was a tyrannical sacrist at King's College who died of fright during a mock trial and execution staged by vengeful students. So, if anything is done, for good or evil, by persons acting together, which cannot be found out, then they are 'art and part of Downie's slaughter'. An old street cry hurled at Aberdeen students was, 'Fa killed Downie?'

The tale by Dundee weaver's son Robert Mudie, who gravitated to journalism in London, first appeared in print in 1825. Downie, he wrote, was abducted by the students and dragged, blindfolded and with his hands bound, into a room hung with black. When his blindfold was removed, he glimpsed the paraphernalia of an execution – the block, a basket of sawdust and an axe wielded by an executioner. Downie's face was covered and he was forced to rest his neck on the block. Moments later Downie was dead.

Downie's Cairn – a nine-feet-high memorial to the fictitious sacrist – was removed from its original site at Berryden in 1926 to a leafy spot at Tillydrone where it can still be seen. An inscription reads, 'I cannot tell how the truth may be; I say the tale as t'was said to me.' Downie's Howe (or Grave), a green mound in a hollow in Kittybrewster, was believed to be where the sacrist was buried in secret.

In the autumn of 1852, Downie's Howe was within sight of a house where one of Aberdeen's most brutal crimes occurred. But, unlike the Downie legend, there was no mystery. Widow Ross and her six-year-old grandson were the innocent victims of the 'monster', George Christie, who slaughtered them in their cottar-house, a short distance from the tollbar at Kittybrewster, then just beyond the city boundary.

Downie died of heart failure when his 'executioner' flicked a wet cloth across the back of his neck. But Christie (51), a big, strong six-footer, swung a real axe. A native of Skene, he served twenty-seven years in the Bengal Artillery but lost his shilling-a-day pension after being jailed for sixty days for robbery of silver plate at Murtle House in Milltimber.

Barbara Barron or Bannochie or Ross, who was in her fifties, earned her living as a cow-feeder. She kept three cows and sold their milk and she also had a few pigs. Christie, as fate would have it, threshed corn in a barn immediately adjoining her humble home. The farmer, Peter McRobbie, had hired Forbes Humphrey to thresh his crop of bere (barley) and Humphrey had subcontracted the work to Christie and another man named James Sangster. The woman earned extra for feeding the threshers in her kitchen. Foolishly, she counted her earnings in front of Christie and, on the Saturday before the crime, he overheard her say she was going to sell her two pigs. No doubt his eyes gleamed at the prospect of what they would fetch at market. He laid his plans. At 8 p.m. on Monday 4 October 1852, Christie had been in Aberdeen when he set off on foot for Kittybrewster, informing an acquaintance in Virginia Street that he had left something behind in the barn (it approximately stood in the area of present-day Lilybank Place).

Widow Ross, as she was known, was at home with her grandson, John Louden, whose seaman father lived in the vicinity of Hangman's Brae. At nine o'clock, McRobbie walked half a mile from his farm at Sunnyside to the barn. He was unhappy with the progress of the threshing and intended to sack Humphrey and his men. The barn was locked so he called at the cottar-house as he knew Widow Ross had the key. There was a light in the kitchen and he saw Christie putting a screen in place. As McRobbie entered the kitchen, Christie blew out a lighted candle. He asked for the key to the barn. Christie, a coarse and sullen individual, asked who wanted it and the farmer replied, 'Peter McRobbie wants it.' By the glow of the fire, he thought he saw two pairs of legs sprawled across the fireplace. At the same time, he heard a 'snoring' sound like that of a drunken person lying on their back.

McRobbie did not confront Christie but took the key without comment. Later, in court, he told the judge he did not wish to pry. 'If there was any correspondence between him and her, it was a delicate matter to interfere,' was how he put it. But Widow Ross did not drink nor did she keep bad company.

McRobbie, his suspicions aroused, went to the house of neighbour William Grant, who farmed Muiryfold, and together they returned to speak to Christie. They asked about the groaning from inside the house and Christie replied, 'The boy had a sair belly.' The two men kept a close watch as Christie stepped back inside the house but, within moments, he reappeared. He had a bundle under his arm and, after locking the door, walked off whistling. As he passed by, he commented on the weather, saying that it looked like more rain.

McRobbie and Grant returned to the darkened cottage but their cries and knocking on the door and window got no response so they decided to get help from the Footes who lived nearby. Watchman Richardson of the County Police, who was stationed up the brae at Printfield, was summoned and used a whin hoe to force open the door. They were met with a horrific sight. The place resembled a slaughterhouse. The floor was slicked with gore and both Mrs Ross and the boy had been 'frightfully gashed and mangled' by a woodman's axe, which lay on the floor between their bodies. The woman had been struck nine times, her grandson five. His body was still warm. In the house of blood they found smashed and blood-smeared furniture and freshly baked oatcakes. Richardson left several persons at the scene before informing Mr Simpson, the procurator fiscal in Aberdeen. He then set off with fellow watchman, James Cran of the County Police, and night-watch patrolman Nicol, of the city's police, to find Christie. They traced him through Humphrey.

It was half past midnight when they found Christie, eating Widow Ross's oatcakes and drinking with his woman, who was called either Marshall or Connel, in his house in the Lower Denburn. He was drunk and confused – but he knew why the policemen had called and, on being charged with the crime, he denied it. He was searched and a purse containing 14s 6d in silver coins and a gold ring, which belonged to the deceased woman, were found in his pockets. Other items belonging to Widow Ross were recovered later from a pawnbroker's shop and Christie was identified as the customer.

He was taken to the watch-house in Huxter Row for further questioning and, while there, he made an obscure remark, saying, 'This should have been done long ago.' Whether he referred to the crime or to his own imprisonment is unclear and his inquisitors did not press him to explain. There were bloodstains on his shoes, the legs of his trousers and the cuffs of his shirt.

Two days before Christmas Day 1852, Christie stood trial for double murder at the High Court of Justiciary in Edinburgh. When the Lord Justice Clerk, who sat with two other judges, asked how he pled, the prisoner replied, 'Innocent, my Lord.' Christie presented a 'dogged, sullen and unfeeling out-look', reported the *Aberdeen Journal* and only when the evidence touched on gory details did he betray any emotion by sighing deeply. In his declaration read to the court, he admitted that he had been at the cottar-house on the Monday night and that he saw Widow Ross. Asked if he had struck either of the deceased and had stolen the purse, he had declined to answer. Christie's counsel, Mr Crauford, argued that the real killer could have fled the scene before Christie arrived and was tempted to commit theft. Christie remained calm and composed during most of the seven-hour trial and on receiving the guilty verdict and sentence.

The Lord Justice Clerk placed the black cap on his head and said:

> In respect of the verdict above recorded, the Lords Justice Clerk, Lords Cowan and Lord Anderson, discern and adjudge you, the said George Christie, to be carried to the bar of the prison in Edinburgh, and under sure guard to be transmitted to the prison of Aberdeen, therein to be detained, and fed on bread and water only, till the 13th of January next, and between 8 and 10 of the forenoon of that day, ordain the said George Christie to be taken out of the said prison to the common place of execution, to be hanged by the neck on a gibbet till you be dead; and ordain your body to be buried within the precincts of the prison; and may God Almighty have mercy upon your soul.

It was a perfect day for a hanging. The *Aberdeen Herald* reporter wrote a graphic description of the scene:

The morning was intensely cold, the frost being keener than it had been during the season. There was scarcely a breath of wind and the smoke of the city hung over it like a mortcloth, increasing the darkness by the heavy clouds in the atmosphere.

In a bid to cheat the hangman, the condemned man tried to starve himself to death but was persuaded by his spiritual advisers to give up after three days. On the eve of his execution, he had eaten heartily but had spent a sleepless night pacing his cell while trying to find solace in the Bible. At five in the morning, he drank a glass of wine and managed to eat a light breakfast before the bearded William Calcraft, the celebrated public hangman, appeared in the cell. Calcraft, an executioner since 1829, was paid a guinea a week by the City of London and a guinea for every execution. He was the first English hangman to work in Scotland and this was only his second execution north of the border.

At 8.10 a.m., thousands of pairs of eyes (it was estimated the crowd numbered about 8,000) focused on Christie, whose gait gave a clue to his military background as he walked, arms pinioned, to the scaffold. On its way from the East Jail, the gloomy procession, which consisted of Prison Governor Chalmers, warders and ministers, passed through the courthouse building. There, it halted briefly in front of an assembly led by the Lord Provost. When Christie was asked if he wished to say anything, he replied feebly, 'No, nothing.' Asked if he was quite ready, he said, 'Yes.'

Scribes noted there were fewer females than usual among the spectators, who were prevented from approaching the gallows by a double barricade. In later times, a venerable octogenarian who witnessed public hangings in Aberdeen would recall, 'You couldna' get a richt sicht o' him unless you was close in by.' Christie kept his composure but it was noticed by reporters that he seemed 'much emaciated' since the trial, 'his whole person appearing to be shrunk, but his mind was evidently collected and even composed, and his bearing was respectful and resigned.'

Journalist William Carnie, who took down the felon's dying declaration for posterity, recalled years later, 'Christie had few sympathisers. The Kittybrewster murder of an old woman and young child was unprovoked, a cruel deed.'

On the drop Calcraft asked the condemned man to signal with a white napkin when ready. Christie, showing great stoicism, asked Calcraft, 'Are you ready?' The hangman replied, 'Yes.' and Christie spoke for the last time, 'Now, gentlemen, I'm quite ready.' He then, with deliberate movement of his hand, threw down the napkin. He died almost without a struggle. But, as the drop fell with a loud crash, a woman, perhaps Christie's paramour, emitted a wild shriek. His body hung for an hour before it was cut down and buried in the East Jail.

But Christie did confess to the murders. He told the prison chaplain, Rev. Mr Baxter, that, on the fateful evening, he had failed to get money owed to him by Humphrey and had proceeded to Widow Ross's to collect a flagon and bag he had left there. He found Mrs Ross milking a cow in the byre and waited until she returned to the house. But she refused to hand over the items until he settled a debt – he owed her money for milk – and he flew into a rage and 'smashed her'. He was also deeply troubled by the murder of the boy. 'He appeared to be anxious to avoid even thinking of it', reported the *Aberdeen Journal*. 'The account he eventually gave was that the innocent creature was continually running between him and his grandmother, and that he, possessed at the time of the spirit of a fiend, in a moment struck him down and killed him.'

13

IT'S A RIOT!

King George III's birthday celebrations on Friday 4 June 1802 began with a bang. Three musket volleys – with blank cartridges – were fired at noon in the barrack yard at Castlehill. The joyous occasion ended in drunken confusion ten hours later when the campaign-hardened troops, fresh from quelling Irish rebels, turned their guns on the citizens of Aberdeen. They did not fire blanks.

The King's birthday had dawned on a bright and optimistic note as the town's apprentices marched through the streets with drums beating and colours and insignia streaming. That evening, the new commanding officer of the Ross and Cromarty Rangers, Lieutenant Colonel George Mackenzie, and his fellow officers attended a civic banquet in the town hall, given by Provost James Hadden of Persley and magistrates. They were regally entertained in the old town house, which adjoined the tolbooth jail, directly opposite the Plainstones, a raised platform of granite slabs, extending from the Exchange coffee house to the market cross where, on market days, fish-wives and pedlars sold their wares and wealthy merchants did business on foot.

In the Castlegate, men 'of the lower order' and boys gathered in search of mischief. Merchant John Garioch described how the crowd were 'throwing dirt, wet straw, and garbage, but no stones, at people passing upon the street, sometimes at citizens, sometimes at the military, and sometimes at each other'. Fireworks and dead cats added to the horseplay. The abuse was aimed at garrison troops, commanded by a drunken Ensign John Lanigan in the *corps de garde*, a small guardhouse. Insults were traded and, shortly after, Captain Felix Macdonogh, who had been indulging in civic hospitality, appeared at the guardhouse. He joined in the high spirits of the crowd by bowing and doffing and waving his hat in the air. He cheered loudly and even shook hands with his tormentors but would later chase them with a drawn sword.

When Colonel Mackenzie appeared, he was hopelessly drunk and supported by two officers who had prevented him from plunging head-long down the tolbooth stairs. He fell in the street more than once. Amid hoots of laughter, the commanding officer staggered to the guardhouse. He was humiliated. A man in a sailor's suit shook his fist in Mackenzie's florid face and shouted, 'Damn you! I have served my king and country, and have done more for both than you have!' Mackenzie ordered him locked up in the guardhouse although the order was later rescinded in a bid to ease the growing tension. The yellow tunics and faces of the soldiers were smeared in mud hurled by the crowd. Mackenzie would later claim he was struck in the face by a stone but, after ordering Macdonogh to call out the regiment from the barracks, he staggered back to his quarters and was never seen again that night.

Before Macdonogh reached the barracks, he met the regiment under arms and on the march. He took command of the troops who positioned themselves across the Castlegate. They faced the crowd with muskets and bayonets fixed. The captain gave the order, 'With powder and ball, prime and load.' He repeated the order twice more and soon after gave the order to open fire.

Innocent bystanders were caught in a blizzard of bullets, which pep-pered the doors, windows and walls of surrounding property. Provost Hadden and some magistrates rushed out of the town hall when the troops opened up. At the door of the town house, the horrified provost watched as one casualty, a mason named Thomas Milne, was carried away. He ordered the town sergeants to arrest whoever was in charge. The provost accosted Sergeant Andrew Mackay and ordered him to send his men back to the barracks. Mackay refused to obey, saying, 'I don't care a single farthing either for the provost or any of the magistrates.' Provost Hadden showed the recalcitrant Mackay his gold chain of office, then struck him saying, 'Will you obey that, sir?'

The troops eventually retired to the east end of the Castlegate, head-ing for the barracks. But, as they filed out of the marketplace, the crowd began taunting the soldiers. Mackay cried, 'Damn the rebels— let us be at them!' and the troops suddenly rushed back and resumed firing, causing more mayhem. They showed no mercy and struck out with musket butts and fixed bayonets.

John Ross, a private in the local rifle corps, fell dead on the Plainstones with a bullet under his left eye. A barber's boy, William Gibb, was fatally wounded a few feet away. John Moir, another youngster, also died of his wounds. The fourth fatality was Thomas Milne. At least ten persons were injured.

Provost Hadden had a drunken Colonel Mackenzie brought to him and charged him and his men with murder. Mackenzie, Captain Macdonogh and six other soldiers were placed in custody. He also warned the colonel to confine his regiment to barracks. That night the safety of the burgh was in the hands of veteran Aberdonians who had served with the local volunteer force.

After considering the prisoners' precognitions, Charles Hope, Lord Advocate, decided not to bring them to trial and they were liberated. Aberdeen was outraged and its leading citizens helped defray the costs of a private prosecution. On 6 January 1803, Colonel Mackenzie, Captain Macdonogh and Sergeants Mackay and Alexander Sutherland, went on trial at the High Court of Justiciary in Edinburgh, accused of his murder. Ensign Lanigan absconded and was outlawed.

Mackenzie blamed the council's generous hospitality for his condition. He did not recollect ordering Macdonogh to call out the regiment or giving him any order to fire. He had been injured in the affray and had retired to his quarters. Macdonogh declared that, when he gave his men the order to prime and load, he believed they only had blank cartridges. He never gave the order to fire. Ensign Lanigan had been too drunk to restrain the guard and Macdonogh himself was hurt while trying to disarm them.

After four days, the jury returned a unanimous verdict – Mackenzie and Macdonogh were found not guilty and the libel case against the two sergeants was not proven. The public-spirited Aberdonians were £900 out of pocket. It was a whitewash.

At midnight, four days after what was now being dubbed 'The Plainstones Massacre', the Ross and Cromarty Rangers, each man in his stocking feet, sneaked out of Aberdeen and headed north, one column taking the road to Oldmeldrum and the other to Ellon. No colours flew and their fifes and drums remained silent. The regiment disbanded in Inverness on 27 July 1802.

King George's birthday celebrations in Aberdeen had brought the worst out in people.

In 1815, an unruly mob of five hundred laid siege to Meggie Dickie's 'house of bad fame' in Justice Street. Meggie, real name Margaret Hall or Dick, who was the subject of an earthy street ballad, ran 'The White Ship', a popular haunt of troops quartered in the barracks close by. The riot erupted on the evening of Monday 5 June when troublemakers were barred from entry. The mob smashed down the front door then systematically ransacked the greater part of the house. A bonfire was made of the furniture and other items thrown into the street. Meggie and her girls were roughly manhandled in the course of the riot which was eventually quelled by civil and military force.

At the Autumn Circuit Court in Aberdeen, the ringleaders, John Douglas, Donald McKay, Arthur Smollet and Alexander Burr, said to be young men of an unblemished character, denied charges of mobbing, rioting and assault. Because of the darkness and confusion on the night of the riot, identification by witnesses of some of the prisoners proved somewhat contradictory. The jury found Douglas, McKay and Smollet guilty of mobbing and actively assisting the mob. McKay was acquitted of assaulting Meggie Dickie. Burr was found not guilty and dismissed from the bar. Lord Succoth sentenced Douglas to transportation 'beyond the seas' for seven years and McKay and Smollet were given a year's hard labour in the Bridewell.

Margaret Creek's brothel near the Justice Port was the scene of 'The Murder of the Black Drummer' on 3 September 1807. John Simpson was in town to drum up recruits for the 29th Regiment of Foot but had made an enemy of the Argyllshire Militia. He was a bare-fisted boxer of note and had thrashed several militiamen in the ring. It was said he had accidentally killed one of them in a fight. A group of militiamen tried to force entry into the house after hearing Simpson, who was inside, calling for booze. A window was smashed and the black drummer and a companion rushed outdoors spoiling for a fight.

Simpson was struck down by a heavy stone and collapsed. He was dragged from the house and beaten and stabbed on the head and body with bayonets. One thrust in the back pierced his heart. Although a great number of soldiers were present, only three were arrested. At the Winter Circuit Court in January 1808, Daniel McPherson, James Graham and Donald McCallum went on trial for murder. The credibility of Peter Skinner, a thief, and Margaret Creek weakened the Crown's case and the libel against the prisoners was not proven.

Being a seaport and garrison town, Aberdeen had a profusion of brothels and streetwalkers in the middle of the nineteenth century. One of the largest establishments was Morris O'Connor's in Frederick Street, which housed thirty-four women. John Chisholm's brothel at the rear of Weigh-house Square at the harbour bore the saucy soubriquet, the 'Dundee Dock'. Trouble was never far away.

On a dark wintry night in February 1845, off-duty members of the 88th Regiment (Connaught Rangers), accompanied by a number of prostitutes from Shore Brae, marched down Marischal Street, smelling of drink and seeking trouble. On reaching Bannerman's Bridge, which was replaced in 1984, they pelted pedestrians in Virginia Street below with stones and other missiles. An angry crowd locked horns with the soldiers. Police, reinforced by 'specials' from the Shore Porters, showed up. The soldiers beat a hasty retreat to Castlehill Barracks, leaving several of their comrades in the custody of the law. The situation grew serious when reinforcements arrived from the barracks. They were armed with rifles with fixed bayonets. After seven soldiers were released into the custody of their comrades, a crisis was averted. The disgraced soldiers were treated leniently by the Police Court and, less than three months later, the regiment packed its kitbags and sailed for Enniskillen.

Around 1830, an Aberdeen mob besieged another well-known brothel, Salmon Meg's, near the junction of St Nicholas Street and Union Street. The house was stripped of its furniture and *The Black Kalendar of Aberdeen* describes how a vandal 'bestrode Margaret's eight day clock, as it lay on its back unconsciously on the street, and, with a good axe in his hand, deliberately hewed it into pieces'.

The dark frowning front of the new Aberdeen Anatomical Theatre in St Andrew's Street bore three false church-looking windows to discourage snoopers and the only daylight leaked through windows at the back and a glass dome on the roof. The building, dubbed the 'Burking Hoose' by locals, was run by Dr Andrew Moir, the Aberdeen-born extra-mural lecturer, whose influential friends had supported him financially. At the beginning of December 1831, only weeks after Dr Moir delivered his first lecture, the *Aberdeen Journal* reported the execution of Bishop and Williams at Newgate, London. They had copied the gruesome activities of Burke and Hare, the Irish labourers who murdered sixteen derelicts in Edinburgh and sold their cadavers for dissection. The same edition reported the alleged attempt by a pair of well-dressed young men to 'burke' (to murder by smothering) two boys in John Street, just yards from Dr Moir's unpopular establishment. No violence was involved. The strangers had asked the boys to run an errand but they took fright and fled. The activities of local body-snatchers were still fresh in the memory and churchyards were still being guarded. 'This is the boys' simple statement, and the readers may make any comment on it they choose,' declared the newspaper.

The 'Burking Hoose' stood on open ground at the west end of the street and, since it had opened, people in the neighbourhood had complained of a stench wafting from the back of the property. At 2 p.m. on Monday 19 December 1831, a dog, tearing at the loose soil, unearthed something grisly. Curious children called over two young tannery workers and, within minutes, a small crowd had gathered. The tanners dug up fragments of a human body. A scribe from the *Journal* hurried to the scene and later reported, 'The smell was quite sickening, and portions of skulls, bones and entrails were lying about!'

The furious crowd milled outside the building as two men forced their way into Dr Moir's lecture room. He and his faithful students were beaten and kicked as they retreated to a smaller room and locked the door behind them. They managed to make their escape by a window but some troublemakers chased Dr Moir as far as his lodgings at 63 Guestrow.

Back at the 'Burking Hoose', the crowd, now 100 strong, found three corpses, stretched out on wooden boards. The bodies were in various stages of dissection – one had half its skull removed. The mob had swollen in size and its mood grew uglier when the bodies were carried on makeshift stretchers to the Drum's Aisle in St Nicholas Kirk. 'Burn the hoose – doon wi' the burkin' shop!' screamed the mob and attempts were made to set fire to the building.

In Guestrow, a stone-hurling crowd smashed the windows of Dr Moir's lodgings. To draw their attention away from the house, he exited by a back window and slipped through the graveyard into the gathering gloom. It was later rumoured that he had hidden under a table stone. Suddenly the sky to the north-west was an angry red. Piles of timber, shavings, fir and tar barrels, left by tradesmen working on the building, had been set alight. The despised anatomical theatre was ablaze. The mob went berserk, grabbing planks to use as levers to undermine and topple the walls.

Provost James Hadden (Hadden Street is named after him), who had confronted the drunken Ross and Cromarty Rangers at the beginning of the century, was back in office for the fourth and final time and he arrived on the scene with magistrates, town sergeants and a posse of special policeman. He made a half-hearted attempt to read the Riot Act but his words were drowned by loud cheers. Great tongues of fire licked the darkness. Sensing the mob might turn their attention to the Medical Society's Hall in King Street, the provost sent word to the garrison at Castlehill. But the soldiers of the 79th Cameron Highlanders played no part in quelling the riot. They marched into the grounds of near-by Gordon's Hospital by a far gate where they remained. A second detachment guarded Schoolhill.

The *Journal* estimated a crowd of 20,000 jammed the streets around the blazing building. A fire engine arrived but the crew's efforts were hampered by the crowd and the fact that there was no water available. Two walls were torn down, leaving the gables and the roof to form a spectacular burning arch. At 8 p.m., these collapsed with a loud roar to the delight of the spectators. Dr Moir's dream was a smouldering ruin.

'A Burker, a Burker, doon wi' the bloody rascal!' one group screamed as they chased a student. He was forced to take refuge in a house in Schoolhill before jumping from a rear window. One student, James Polson, was beaten and only the intervention of the constabulary saved him from serious injury. The riot was a controversial topic. Dr Moir accused the *Aberdeen Journal* of 'befriending incendiarists' but the weekly paper, which had dealt harshly with the bodysnatchers in the past, said the incident might serve as a 'warning' to him.

Three men arrested during the riot appeared at the Circuit Court in Aberdeen on 24 April 1832. Alexander Murray, flesher, of West North Street and George Sharpe, blacksmith, of Schoolhill, both Aberdeen, and

Alexander Allan, a private in the Fusilier Guards, were charged with mobbing and rioting, wilful fire raising and assault. The advocate depute remarked on the extenuating circumstances which enabled him to accept a modified plea of mobbing and rioting and to drop the capital charge of wilful fire raising and assault on Dr Moir and Polson. He said the incident appeared to have been due to the carelessness on the part of the medical men. The court accepted that the accused were not the ring-leaders. Sharpe claimed he had gone to the anatomical theatre to see if he could find the body of his grandmother who had been buried a few weeks earlier. The prisoners were each jailed for twelve months, to be served in the less harsh conditions at the Bridewell, rather than in the East Jail. A careless porter was blamed for burying the body parts in the backyard of the anatomical theatre.

After Moir and his backers won damages of £235 from the town council over its destruction, he rebuilt his shattered career. He was soon lecturing in new premises to packed classes. He died in 1844 at the early age of thirty-eight. His grave is marked with a table stone close to the Schoolhill gate of St Nicholas Kirkyard.

The Bon Accord Music Hall in St Nicholas Lane, Aberdeen, had promised loyal patrons that Friday 5 April 1889, would be a 'Nicht of Nichts'. But the benefit gala performance for manager Mr H. H. Bromhead was to live up to its heady promotion for the wrong reasons. A sparkling bill with a 'thousand and one attractions' promised to take the minds of the audience off their daily drudgery. In the wings waited (so it was advertised) twenty-three star turns, forty star artistes and Sam Picton, manager of the city's Alhambra Varieties, staging his theatre's successful comedy sketch, *Tickle Me*, to round off the fun.

But the mood of the patrons grew ugly when the sketch was abandoned because a principal actor had left early, believing the farce would not go ahead because of the lateness of the hour. Booing and hissing erupted when the gallant Mr Bromhead appeared before the footlights and volunteered a song instead. He began reading the ditty but his efforts were drowned by the ranting audience and, after one verse, he slunk from the stage.

When the band struck up the national anthem, it was a signal for mindless hooliganism. Youths hurled music stands and chairs on to the stage and the air became a blizzard of music sheets. The musicians fled as the hall was plunged into darkness. Folding seats were ripped from their hinges and also flung on the stage. Gas brackets were wrenched from walls, allowing gas to escape. As the mob poured into St Nicholas Lane, picture frames near the pay box were shattered and a glass light globe over the front door was smashed.

Baton-wielding police entered the darkened theatre and rounded up some of the culprits but the night ended with the Bobbies being hounded back to Lodge Walk by a howling mob. Three youths appeared in a crowded Police Court next day. They were charged with lawless and disorderly behaviour and causing a disturbance. One was cleared but his companions were each fined one guinea or ten days in jail.

The Alhambra in Market Street packed them in during the final week of its season and, to mark Sam Picton's benefit night, the company performed the 'screaming absurdity', *Tickle Me*!

The curtain was rung down on the Bon Accord Music Hall. It never reopened after the riot. The former variety house and one-time United Free Church stood next door to the Prince of Wales public house until it was demolished in 1993.

14

THE ST FERGUS MYSTERY

To the casual observer, it might seem that time has stood still in the village of Kirktown of St Fergus, five miles north of the Buchan seaport of Peterhead. But a bloody episode took place here that shocked Victorian Scotland and it remains part of local folklore.

On a rainy evening on Saturday 19 November 1853, widower William McDonald (29), farm labourer, left his mother's thatched croft at Burnside to walk two miles through fields to the Kirktown, where he had a six o'clock appointment with his friend, the village doctor. McDonald, hale and hearty and engaged to be married, next appeared around seven in the shop of James Smith, the local cartwright, and inquired about an order he had placed for a pair of haims (harness accoutrements), a grub-harrow for turnips and some paling. McDonald, who was sober, exchanged banter with friends in the shop and left at around half-past seven, remarking, 'It's getting late. I've need to be awa.' It was the last time they would see him alive.

After an anxious night waiting for William's return, his widowed mother and his sister, Agnes, urged his brother, Robert (19), to rise and go looking for him. On that Sabbath morning, he found his brother's body in a shallow ditch in a field owned by McDonald's friend, Dr William Smith (33), and 500 yards from the house where the physician lived with his wife and family. The body lay in an inch of water at the bottom of the ditch. There was a bullet hole in the right cheek and the deceased's face was blackened with gunpowder. About four feet from the corpse's head lay a pistol.

A horrified Robert ran to fetch Dr Smith. He was not at home so the boy left a message with his wife before returning to the death scene. Shortly afterwards, Dr Smith and James Pirrie, veterinary surgeon, found Robert weeping over his brother's body. The doctor threw up his hands and exclaimed, 'God preserve us.' He picked up the pistol and said, 'That's the thing that's done it!', leaving no doubt in the minds of the witnesses that McDonald had committed suicide.

When McDonald's body was carried to a nearby house there was no gunpowder or shot found on him and his jacket pockets were too small to conceal a pistol. A snuffbox and watch were found and McDonald carried no money so robbery was ruled out.

Dr Smith, who had been the McDonalds' family doctor for the eight years, met the family minister, Rev. Alexander Moir, of the United Free Church at Shielhill, and they went to break the tragic news at Burnside. Moir asked, 'Well, doctor, has this happened by accident or design?' Dr Smith said that McDonald had shot himself. When the doctor told the distraught mother that her son had taken his own life and had either suffocated or drowned in the ditch, she refused to believe him. William had never owned a pistol and Mrs Amelia McDonald (54) suspected foul play. The doctor warned her 'that she would get into trouble for the way she was speaking'. She asked Dr Smith if William had kept his appointment with him the previous night but he denied that there had been any such arrangement. It transpired that, despite their difference in social standing in the eyes of Victorian society, the doctor and the farm labourer had met regularly for a month before the shooting. But, before the minister helped Mrs McDonald to bed, the doctor remarked, 'If Boyd heard what had happened, he would be out.', a reference to the Peterhead-based procurator fiscal. The local constable, John Hunter, asked Dr Smith to fill out the death certificate and this he did, inferring the fatal shooting had been self-inflicted.

It read:

I do hereby certify, on soul and conscience, that I was called upon this morning about half-past 9 o'clock, by Robert McDonald, to see his brother William, who was found in a field near St Fergus, and who had received a shot from a pistol in the right cheek, taking an upward and backward direction. There was a small quantity of blood coming from the ear and nostrils, the face completely covered with powder, so that the pistol must have been close to him, and from the direction it takes, I infer it is not likely to have been done by any other than deceased. W. Smith, M.R.C.S.L.

The initials stood for Member of the Royal College of Surgeons of London. The Kirktown's population of fewer than 300 was agog.

Dr Smith, who had arrived in Kirktown twelve years earlier, took charge of the funeral arrangements, buying a shroud from Alexander McLeod, the village merchant, and ordering a coffin from Smith the wright.

On the Monday morning, Andrew Boyd arrived in Kirktown of St Fergus to examine the locus along with two surgeons, Dr Comrie and Dr Gordon, who also carried out a post-mortem examination. An on-the-spot inspection showed no sign of a struggle. The impression of the body could be clearly made out at the bottom of the ditch. They found a bloodstain on the west bank. The post-mortem result showed that death had been instantaneous. A bullet fired from a distance of between three and thirteen inches from the face had lodged in the brain. Suffocation and drowning was ruled out. The doctors could only account for the position of the body in two ways. Firstly, McDonald could have shot himself while he sat or lay down in the ditch. And, secondly, he could have been placed there by someone else who had first shot him. Dr Gordon, a retired naval surgeon, who lived in the twin hamlet of New St Fergus, had been friendly with the deceased and he did not believe William McDonald would have considered suicide. But, ultimately, the doctors were unable to say for sure whether death was caused by violence or suicide.

That same morning Rev. Moir pressed Dr Smith for more details of the shooting. He replied that the deceased's snuff box was streaked with gunpowder but Moir could find none. The doctor claimed there had been a 'hurry', a quarrel, within the McDonald family which had preyed on the affable William's mind. Moir was unaware of any feud involving William. Mrs McDonald, her family and the dead man's fiancée, Mary Slessor, a domestic servant from Longside, would later hotly dispute the insinuation.

The suspicious minister wanted the affair properly investigated. He said it was a mystery that the body had been found so quickly in such a lonely spot. Dr Smith claimed he had been guided there by the sound of Robert grieving. If it was foul play, then the murderer had stalked McDonald from the village, suggested Moir, who then asked bluntly, 'Where were you on Saturday night, doctor?' Dr Smith proceeded to rattle off the names of a number of patients he had called on in the village.

Dr Smith had planned for the funeral to take place on the Tuesday but it was postponed till the next day. He was not among the mourners. He was already under lock and key in Peterhead jail and, after appearances before Sheriff Skelton, the prisoner was transferred to Calton Jail in Edinburgh. His trial for murder should have been heard at the High Court of Justiciary in Edinburgh on Monday 23 March 1854 (it was switched from Aberdeen in the interests of justice) but it was postponed after a juror broke down. The diet was continued until Wednesday 12 April, with the Lord Justice Clerk and Lords Cowan and Handyside on the bench. The courtroom, noted a journalist, was 'filled by a most respectable audience, including a considerable number of ladies'. The trial occupied three days and, as was the custom, the adjournments were short, resulting in marathon sessions.

Was McDonald shot dead by a trusted friend or did he commit suicide? That was the dilemma which faced the jury. Dr Smith had a motive. He had insured McDonald's life with three insurance companies for £2,000, with him being the chief beneficiary. McDonald had cooperated, believing he could borrow money against the policies – enough, perhaps, to buy a farm. When an insurance agent expressed astonishment at McDonald's naivety, he replied, 'The doctor's a fine chiel and I have always done as he bade me do.' The largest premium expired five days after the shooting.

On the day of his arrest, Dr Smith shared a grim jest with a farmer friend, James Greig, who had been questioned by the fiscal about the insurances. The doctor was forced to admit that these existed and Greig remarked, 'They'll blame you for pistolling McDonald!' He agreed.

Dr Smith's defence weighed heavily upon alibi and much emerged about his comings and goings before and after the shooting, which had taken place at about 7.35 p.m. The bellman, William Fraser, who lived on the Netherhill road, had just left home for the parish church to toll the nightly ceremony of curfew at 8 p.m. curfew, when he saw a flash to the south-west and heard the crack of a pistol.

McDonald had gone to St Fergus, south-east of Burnside, to meet the doctor at 6 p.m. The rendezvous was supposed to take place at the doctor's stable door. But Dr Smith was treating a servant at the parish church manse, where he stayed till a few minutes to seven. He then returned to his own home, which stood opposite McLeod's shop at the junction of the main street and the Netherhill road, and, after some chores, he resumed his calls. He would visit three other homes in the close vicinity. At the time of the shooting, the doctor declared he was visiting a patient, Bella Anderson, McLeod's neighbour. On arrival, he made great play with a candle of drawing her attention to the time on her clock – twenty-five minutes to eight. She did not tell him the clock was then quarter of an hour slow and it was actually ten minutes to eight. So there was a gap of fifteen minutes for which the good doctor could not account. While being held at Mrs Robertson's village inn, the furtive doctor asked the landlady's daughter to go and speak to Miss Anderson. He said that, if she could persuade Miss Anderson to say that she remembered the time of his call was 7.35 p.m., 'all would be right'. Miss Anderson refused.

The bullet that killed McDonald matched the pistol that was found near his body.

But to whom did it belong? In the weeks before the shooting, Dr Smith had been seen practising with a pistol in a field and near his stable door. A pistol with a broken trigger and a small quantity of gunpowder were found in the doctor's house by the sheriff's officer but this was not the fatal weapon.

In August 1853, Dr Smith had bought a second pistol in a shop in Peterhead. James Walker, the assistant who served him, said Dr Smith had cocked and snapped it and said it would do. He put it into his pocket in 'a very hurried manner', paid for it and left. But, when shown the gun that killed McDonald, Walker was unable to identify it as the one he had sold Smith.

Before dark on the day of the shooting, Dr Smith bought two ounces of gunpowder from McLeod, who had sold him McDonald's shroud. An assistant had sold him percussion caps (two dozen for a penny) the previous summer. He told McLeod he needed the gunpowder to make up ointment for a female patient. The merchant had been well acquainted with the deceased and he had never sold him gunpowder.

The defence produced their trump card with the last witness of the trial. Adam Gray, the brother of the provost of Peterhead, created a mild sensation when he claimed he had sold the fatal weapon to William McDonald. He identified it from a notch on the stock. In September 1848, McDonald asked if he had an old gun that he could sell to frighten rooks from the crops. Gray, a retired auctioneer, recollected an old pistol he had bought while passing through Glasgow. He sold it to the deceased for four shillings and sixpence. The deceased took it away with him and paid for it the following month. The witness produced a notebook with the entry of the transaction. The prosecution was not impressed with his bookkeeping methods but he told the solicitor general, 'Everyone keeps a jotter as he likes, it may be a queer book, but it is true.' Gray admitted he had been fined £5 for firing at a fisherman who trespassed on his property. He had known Dr Smith for many years and believed him to be an 'excellent man'. Unless Gray had committed deliberate perjury there was no link between Dr Smith and the pistol that killed McDonald. Gray's evidence would prove conclusive.

The Lord Justice Clerk, in his summing up to the jury, said:

> At an early period of the trial I had taken up the impression that unless there was more evidence brought against the prisoner than appeared likely, there was not enough to infer the guilt of the prisoner or to substantiate the fact that a murder had been committed. Since hearing the case that impression has been strengthened and confirmed.

After only ten minutes, the jury returned a verdict of 'not proven, by a majority'. The judge asked them, 'Perhaps it is right that I should just ask you, in such a case as this, whether the difference of opinion was as to "not proven" or "not guilty"?' The jury foreman replied, 'The difference of opinion was between "guilty" and "not proven", my Lord.' *The Scotsman* newspaper reported that four jurors were in favour of returning a guilty verdict.

A sound like escaping gas greeted the verdict. As Dr Smith stepped away from the bar he was taken aside for his own protection by court officers, an act which touched off a further storm of hissing from the crowded benches. Dr Smith was smuggled out of the courthouse to be reunited with his family. After spending the weekend in Edinburgh, they returned to Aberdeen by steamer and by carriage to St Fergus. According to the 1851 Census, the doctor and his Fraserburgh-born wife, Christian (30), had three children – William (6), Margaret (2) and two-month-old Robert. He farmed thirteen acres and employed a labourer.

News of the verdict was greeted with shocked disbelief in Buchan and there was criticism of the manner in which the trial was conducted. Newspapers ran special editions and the Crimean War took a back seat. The editor of the *Aberdeen Herald* was not surprised by the outcome and had said that through family and other influence the case would, 'by hook or by crook', fail.

Aberdeen chronicler William Carnie said in his memoirs that, although Smith had styled himself 'doctor', he had quit his medical studies at Marischal College without a getting his degree. But this was not so. Smith, an Aberdeenshire farmer's son from Chapel of Garioch, took arts and not medicine and would have had a background in Latin and Greek. In 1835, at the age of fifteen, he enrolled at King's for two years. He enrolled at Marischal College for an additional two but left to become a surgeon's apprentice at the infirmary at Woolmanhill. Around 1841, he moved to St Fergus to assist the local GP, whom he eventually succeeded. He was said to be efficient and was highly respected by the tight-knit community. After the shooting of William McDonald, it was said he had falsely claimed to be London qualified. There is no note of him in the old records kept by the Royal College of Surgeons of England.

Despite his acquittal, he was never able to gain from McDonald's death. He sued the insurance companies but the actions were vigorously defended and he was forced to abandon his claims. St Fergus was deeply divided by the case. The parish minister, Rev. James Robertson, had testified in court to his doctor friend's good character while the Rev. Moir, the Free Kirk minister, had given evidence for the prosecution. But, in the end, Dr Smith was not welcome and left the area. In the Kirktown of St Fergus today, they tell you he fled to Australia.

Adam Gray's brother, Roderick, a solicitor, was provost of Peterhead from 1843 to 1857. Adam, an irascible character, feuded with his brother for many years. When Roderick left a legacy of £10,000 to Aberdeen Royal Infirmary, his relatives, including Adam, contested the will. The case was eventually settled at the Court of Session.

Burnside croft is uninhabited and marooned in a field at South Burnhead farm while the Free Church is a ruin. The Rev. Moir held the charge from 1848 to 1860.

William McDonald is buried in an unmarked grave in Longside Old Churchyard.

Three weeks after Dr Smith's trial, Aberdeenshire was shocked by the brutal murder of bride-to-be Annie Harvey (22), a mill worker at Peterculter, who was found with her throat cut in a ditch at Cults. Her lover, Francis Forbes (27), was arrested and, because of local revulsion, he was tried in Edinburgh. The jury was unconvinced of his guilt and found the charge not proven, a verdict that created renewed indignation.

15

THE LAST DROP

In 1857, the year of the Indian Mutiny and the dramatic murder trial of Madeleine Smith, a wealthy Glasgow architect's daughter acquitted of poisoning her secret lover, the peace and tranquillity of an Aberdeenshire market town was disrupted by two major events within days of each other. One was a regal triumph while the other cast dark clouds of tragedy.

The tragedy in Oldmeldrum centred on a tottering tenement in Weavery Lane where dreams of health, wealth and happiness were hawked. A labourer's wife, Jean Barclay, earned extra coppers foretelling the future in the low-roofed home that also served as her humble shop selling crockery and stoneware. She and her married daughter Mary (35), a stout, ruddy-faced mother of two, had the knack of telling fortunes by reading tea leaves, palms and by the turn of a playing card. Sometimes these sessions spilled into the Sabbath.

Despite their occupation, neither woman could have imagined what fate had in store for them.

Death came in the shape of Mary's thirty-seven-year-old husband, John (Johnny) Booth, a small, dark-browed man with a 'piercing quick eye' and a taste for liquor. Their stormy marriage was blighted by his continual brawling with Mary and her sixty-year-old mother who was a close neighbour. The drink-fuelled rows were blamed on everything from his wife's infidelity to fortune-telling on a Sabbath.

Taunts by fellow hawkers of Mary's unfaithfulness drove Booth to the edge of madness. After peering thunderstruck through a window at Mary making love to a man in bed he attempted suicide. Inflamed with booze he swallowed a bottle of poison in front of the two women and sobbed, 'See I'll not trouble you no more.' But he somehow survived. Booth would later claim he had spied on his mother-in-law in bed with a married man but his accusations were howled down by Jean and her frail, seventy-year-old spouse, James.

Booth was drinking with his cronies at Oldmeldrum on the night of Thursday 21 July 1857, when an argument flared over the subject of his wife's infidelity. Any thoughts he had of travelling with his wares to the Aikey Brae horse fair next day were forgotten in the heat of the moment. It was before 11 p.m. when he arrived home and dragged Mary from her bed. She denied Booth's accusation but he was blind with jealousy. He kept his wares in a box and from it he produced a 'deer knife' – a large, spring-backed clasp knife – and lunged at her, inflicting a minor injury. She ran into the street in her nightdress.

Jean Barclay was not so lucky. She and her husband were in bed when they were disturbed by Mary hammering on the door of their shuttered shop-cum-home. Mary had no sooner blurted out her story when Booth burst open the front door. Armed with a rolling pin, Jean attempted to block Booth's wild charge. She stood between him and her daughter and became the target of his savage knife thrusts. Jean ran out of the door, shouting, 'Mary, rin for yer life, this man has murdered me!' She staggered back into the house and dropped dead. She had been stabbed eight times but the fatal blow went straight to her heart. In the melee, her husband dealt Booth a blow to the head with a shovel, with little effect. The local constable, James Tarves, summoned Dr John Ingram but there was nothing he could do for her. The bloodstained knife was left behind by Booth. But he made no attempt to escape and admitted the crime when arrested in the street by Tarves. He was taken to Carle's Inn (now Morris's Hotel) where he spent the remainder of the night in chains, fettered at the fireplace in an upstairs room.

Newshounds were quick off the mark. When a scribe reached the scene he found old Barclay wandering the lanes near his home 'with his head bent upon his breast and his hands thrust far into his trouser pockets looking like one very cold and dreary though the sun shone and warmly'. He went on to describe how, inside James Barclay's gloomy dwelling, at the back of the rude counter of the small shop, lay Jean's body, 'clothed and bloody as she had fallen with a face as white as the driven snow'. Young James Booth, whose court ordeal had yet to come, and his three-year-old sister cowered on a straw-filled sack, while their mother, stunned into silence by the murder, sat with her back to the front door 'never looking at who passed in or out'.

Aberdeen journalist, William Carnie (1824–1908), a shorthand wizard who sharpened his skills by taking verbatim notes of his minister's sermons, much to the reverend gentleman's chagrin, has also left a poignant description of the scene of the crime. He wrote in his memoirs:

> According to popular rumour, the stabbed woman was the real cause of all the family unhappiness. But the deed was done, and when a couple of hours after the blows had been struck I entered the very humble dwelling situated in a back lane of the village, a little caged bird was singing above the dead woman, singing as blithely as if it had been its native bush.

Almost a quarter of a century after the murder George (Geordie) Webster, a sheriff and criminal officer – 'my tongue runs freest i' the native Doric' – recalled:

> Booth made nae attempt till escape, but loot the constable lay han's on him at ance – I cudna be gotten at the instant. Booth was perfectly frantic at the time against baith his wife and mither-in-law, and said he was sorry he hedna been able to punish the wife as she deserv't – she got only a bit cut aboot the fingers. Hoomsoever, fan the hue an' cry got up, as I was sayin', I got notice in five minutes or so. Gars them tak' Booth to Carle's Inn, an' rins for Dr Ingram at ance. But doctors war o' nae use as far's the injur't 'oman was concern't – she was gone.

Geordie, of whom we will hear more of in the next chapter, fetched a candle and, with the help of his servant lass, went in search of the murder weapon, which he sealed in a bag and labelled. Then it was off in a horse and gig to make his report to the sheriff and fiscal in Aberdeen. He returned to Oldmeldrum to collect Booth and escort him to Aberdeen. They travelled by train to Waterloo Station at the docks. Fearing a mob of onlookers on their arrival, he slipped quietly up by Castlehill Barracks and across the Castlegate to the East Jail.

The Booth's only son, James, who was about nine years old, saw the murder. At the Autumn Circuit Court in Aberdeen, he was too young to take the oath but he told the judges, the Lord Justice Clerk and Lord Deas, that he had been taught to read the Bible and he knew he would be punished by God if he did not speak the truth. After the fatal stabbing, the terrified boy had run from the house, shouting, 'Granny's dead!'

In summing up, the Lord Justice Clerk told the jury it was true there had been no proven enmity on the part of the prisoner toward the deceased. However, he also said that the absence of bad feeling did not necessarily preclude the possibility of murder. His Lordship, after pointing out that a person might deprive another of life by a single stroke of a knife without any evil intent, repeated that, if the jury found any alleviating circumstances in the case, they could return a verdict accordingly. If they thought it was a case to which the plea of culpable homicide did not apply, they could return a verdict of murder.

It took the jury forty minutes to reach a verdict – guilty of murder. Just as the Lord Justice Clerk was about to pronounce doom, Booth, amid considerable excitement from the spectators in court, waved his hand and said, 'Please your worship, I have a word to say if you will permit me.' 'Certainly,' replied the judge.

Booth, pointing dramatically heavenwards, said solemnly, 'I will speak the truth as I shall answer to God.' Tension gripped the courtroom as Booth told of his wife's infidelity and how he had spied as she had 'connection' with a man in bed at his in-laws' house. There was another witness to the affair – a gardener friend, William Saunders, who had asked Booth, 'Can you do nothing? Can you stand that?' A thunderstruck Booth had made no reply. This revelation caused a sensation in court.

Booth told how he had bought a sixpenny worth of poison and 'teemed' a draught sufficient to kill a man, in front of Mary and her mother. But, because he had been drinking booze, he turned violently sick and survived. At the conclusion of his statement, the Lord Justice Clerk placed the black cap on his head and sent Booth to the gallows – the execution was fixed for between eight and ten on the morning of Wednesday 21 October 1857.

Johnny Booth was no ignorant brute and sympathy went out to him from all corners of society and numerous petitions were signed on his behalf. Among his visitors to the condemned cell were his wife Mary, who was born in Daviot, their two youngsters and his father-in-law for whom he had a liking, despite what had gone before. These trysts were described as 'affectionate and touching' and would heal the rift and lead to a touching address by Booth on the scaffold.

Oldmeldrum was still in shock when it heard the joyous news that it was to receive royal visitors. Queen Victoria and Prince Albert and members of their family would pass through the town at the end of their annual pilgrimage to Balmoral. The royals would spend the night at nearby Haddo House, the ancestral home of former Prime Minister Lord Aberdeen, before boarding the London train in Aberdeen the following day. The royal procession would travel from Deeside to Haddo, via Ballater, Tarland, Craigievar, Alford, Inverurie and Oldmeldrum. The October day chosen for the glorious event fell exactly a week before Booth was due to hang.

Oldmeldrum was agog at the news of the royal visit. Sixty special constables, wearing white gloves and carrying batons, controlled the crowd lining the streets. Four elegant arches lined the route through the town. One decorated by a certain sheriff officer drew favourable comments. In 'foul sark' and with the help of two carpenters, Geordie Webster nailed up 250 flags and, within an hour or so, had changed into 'black breeks, wi' a gold lace band' round his hat in time to greet the fiscal and other officials from Aberdeen. Rosettes presented by local ladies rounded off Geordie's outfit.

The Queen was enthralled by the welcome and ordered her coach to drive slowly past the cheering crowds. As the royal party passed Captain Ramsay of Barra at the gates of Meldrum House, the town celebrated in style. A band from Aberdeen serenaded the populace as invited guests drifted into the town hall to drink toasts and make speeches. A spectacular firework display brought a historic day to an end.

The *Aberdeen Journal* ran a highly descriptive article on the royal cavalcade through the countryside and the subsequent junket at Haddo but a short paragraph at the end of the report no doubt sobered readers. It read, 'Up to the moment we write, we regret that there does not appear to be the slightest chance of a reprieve for poor John Booth, whose execution remains for Wednesday first.'

Booth, who had lived on bread and water since the end of his trial, managed to snatch some sleep in the condemned cell. He rose between three and four on the morning of his execution. The day before he had dictated and signed his dying confession. As he washed and dressed, he could hear the thump of hammers as carpenters built his gallows but he made no comment. After prayers with the prison chaplain, Rev. Baxter, and Rev. Lang, the minister of the East Church, he ate breakfast at 6.30 a.m.

A few minutes before eight, a powerfully built man, dressed in black and with flowing white hair and beard to match entered the cell. The man in black was William Calcraft, who was fifty-seven years old at the time. Booth guessed the stranger's identity and insisted he shook hands with the hangman. Calcraft, a kind-hearted man who was fond of children and whose hobby was rabbit-breeding, obliged. He never refused such a request from a condemned man.

Booth had his arms pinioned, perhaps in the act of shaking hands with Calcraft, and was led to the scaffold by a passage from the East Prison. Lord Provost John Webster and the magistrates watched the prisoner come up the passage steps in the old courthouse with a 'light, firm step without the least degree of swagger'. Booth bowed respectfully to the Lord Provost, who asked if he had any last wish and whether or not he wished to make a statement, adding, 'We shall see that it is given to the world.' 'I have given something to Mr Baxter which he will show you,' replied Booth. When Booth said he would address the crowd, the provost suggested that 'it would be right that you should make it very short, John'.

The gallows had been erected directly in front of the old burgh courtroom. A window and the masonry below the sill had been removed so that an open doorway led directly to the scaffold. A crowd of up to 1,800 persons, made up of all ages and sexes, including mothers with babes in arms, pressed forward. The *Aberdeen Free Press* reporter found it a 'humiliating sight'. Calcraft was an object of morbid curiosity. He had arrived in town the previous Saturday and had been spotted on walks, wearing a tall hat, a fob chain and swinging a cane.

A deathly hush fell around the scaffold as Booth made a speech, which was no less gripping than the one he gave to the bench at the end of his trial. 'My friends,' he said, 'you all know what the occasion is for me being here. It is sin. Sin is the great cause of my downfall.' He went on:

> I said a few words in court about my wife and my people, which I hope in your presence now you will omit; as what will a man not say to try and save his life? Then I hope you will mind what you hear from me. Now I bid you all farewell, and may God, in his infinite mercy forgive you, as I expect at this moment He will forgive my transgressions.

The ubiquitous William Carnie stood on the scaffold to record Booth's dying declaration. He wrote in his bulky memoirs years later:

> For the second time the gruesome task of standing beside the hangman fell to me, and there in view of the spectators, I took his dying utterances. They were, mercifully the 'last words' ever spoken publicly from the gallows in our good town.

Those standing on and at the foot of the gallows greeted the end of Booth's confession with a single word, 'Amen!' Calcraft positioned Booth on the drop. When he fitted the noose around the man's neck, a scornful cry of 'Ah!' rose from the spectators. Booth looked calm. The hangman pulled the white nightcap over Booth's face. Booth muttered a short prayer, gave the signal he was ready by dropping a handkerchief and 'the bolt was withdrawn'. After a few convulsive struggles, Johnny Booth was dead.

Meldrum's Geordie Webster was not present at the hanging but an acquaintance, who attended in an official capacity, wrote of the final moments:

> Booth stepped on to the block, and it was then that the crowd, for the first time, fairly got sight of Calcraft as he adjusted his gear, when a savage hiss greeted him. At this significant demonstration the executioner visibly cowered; and from the unenviable point of vantage at Booth's right hand on the scaffold, one could plainly perceive that, despite the dull phlegmatic contour of the official face, and the heavy under jaw, the man at the heart of him was a coward.

(The *Free Press* noted an attempt to 'hoot' Calcraft but otherwise the crowd behaved.)

Booth's body was removed after twenty minutes and buried in the precincts of the East Jail, beside the Boyndlie poisoner James Burnett, James Robb, murderer and rapist, and George Christie, the Kittybrewster murderer. Their initials were inscribed on a wall near their graves. As Booth was cut down, hawkers of literature sold lurid versions of the crime and trashy confessions, complete with illustrations, which had been printed well ahead of the execution. More discerning folk would wait for the local newspapers.

In his official statement, which he gave to the prison chaplain, Booth again stressed the folly of his ways and the innocence of his family. This is what he said:

> The statement which I made in court, at my trial, has given me still, the utmost uneasiness and pain, for what will a man not say and do for his life? And I implore, in the near prospect of death and eternity, that sad speech will be forgotten, and never remembered against my dear wife and children. I do from my heart implore my dear wife to forgive me for whatever I've said or done that has wronged her and I earnestly pray that God may be gracious on to her and the children. Bless them.

What other thoughts flitted through Booth's mind as he stood on the edge of eternity? He was but a short distance from his birthplace in Shore Lane, off the Shiprow. Booth's mother was banished from Aberdeen for some unknown crime. The town hanged her son.

Booth left his mark in local criminal history. He was the last person to be hanged in public in Aberdeen. It would be another 106 years before anyone else died on the scaffold in the city – shotgun murderer Henry John Burnett was executed at Craiginches Prison on 15 August 1963. He was the last person to hang in Scotland.

By a quirk of fate, Calcraft had not seen the last of the Aberdeen gallows or the city itself. In 1865, he came north to hang George Stephen (62), a Port Elphinstone wood merchant, who killed his paramour with an axe in the woods at Thainstone, near Kintore. But Stephen was insane and reprieved. In 1866, the municipal gallows was loaned to two Scottish towns that did not own such a thing. In January, Andrew Brown, who murdered his skipper at sea, was hanged at Montrose and, four months later, poacher Joe Bell was hanged at Perth for murdering a baker's van man with a stolen shotgun near Vicars Bridge at Blairingone, Perthshire. The motive? Robbery. Bell, an amateur poet, posed for his photograph in the condemned cell and ordered prints for his friends and family. Calcraft executed both men.

When Calcraft retired in 1874, the City of London gave the hangman a pension of twenty-five shillings a week for life. He died five years later at the age of seventy-nine.

In 1857, the two star exhibits at Springthorpe's Waxworks in Aberdeen's Mechanics' Hall, in Market Street, were Madeleine Smith and Pierre Emile L'Angelier, her doomed lover. There was no effigy of Johnny Booth. His widow, Mary, remarried.

Scotland's last public execution took place in Dumfries on 12 May 1868, when Robert Smith (19) was hanged for the rape and murder of a nine-year-old girl. By the end of the month, a bill to abolish public hangings had received royal assent. It was agreed that the pageant of death had become a degrading spectacle. George Chalmers, a native of Fraserburgh, was the first culprit to be hanged behind closed doors in Scotland. Chalmers (45) was convicted of the murder of a tollkeeper at Braco, Perthshire, and he was executed by Calcraft at the old County Jail, Perth, on 4 October 1870. As he stood on the trap, the hooded Chalmers called out to the official party, including pressmen, 'I'm quite innocent, and I'll die for it like a man; goodbye to you all for ever more. I'm quite innocent – May God have mercy on me.'

16
THIEF-CATCHER

George Webster was the law in the town and the surrounding country-side. He toted a pistol, hunted criminals on horseback and sometimes travelled hundreds of miles by stagecoach to get his man. And he would boast, 'That's the han' that's grippet seven murderers!'

But 'Geordie' Webster was no Wild West lawman. He was a sheriff and criminal officer, one of a scattered band who kept law and order in rural Scotland before the days of a regular police force. Before the end of the nineteenth century, Sheriff Watson of Aberdeen wrote of early peacekeeping in Aberdeenshire:

> In those days the preservation of the peace of the country was entrusted to a few sheriff's officers, distributed here and there among the large villages; and from 1832 to 1840, nearly the whole criminal work of the large county of Aberdeen was done, and done in a most efficient manner, by George Webster, in Old Meldrum, who apprehended most of the murderers, housebreakers and thieves, then more numerous than they are now.

Geordie loved that. 'No certificate eud weel come ootwith o' that, lat me tell you,' he preened. He was never happier unless he got a felon under lock and key in Aberdeen or, as he described it, 'pitten safe aneth the weather cock'. The weather vane crowned the defunct wardhouse, which had been replaced by the adjoining East Jail in Lodge Walk.

He was based in his native town of Oldmeldrum, where he was born on 4 June 1801. In his colourful memoirs, he wrote:

A place of considerable importance. Mair sae nor Inverurie? Ay, I
sud think sae; Inverurie, royal burgh that it is, an' for a' its upsettin'
noo-a-days, was a mere squattery o' thicket hoosies a hun'er years ago,
fan Meldrum was a sturrin' place wi' a weekly market.

After schooling, his first job was in the stables of the local Barnett's
Inn. He then worked as a groom for General Gordon at Parkhill. His
next employer, Sir John Forbes of Fintray, recommended him for the
'criminal bizness' and, in 1832, he gained his commission as a criminal
officer. King William IV was on the throne. Five years later, when Bailie
Barnett's nerve failed him at the proclamation of Queen Victoria in a
crowded town square, Geordie took over and read the edict in a voice
that 'ye wud 'a heard ilka word o' 't half a mile awa' '. Geordie could
never be accused of hiding his light under a bushel.

On New Year's Day 1833, the new lawman was involved in a thrilling
manhunt. His quarry was a 'terrible hoosebraker' who had plagued the
countryside for the past year. Now he was trying to flee south with his
booty. The pursuit began in earnest at Pitcaple Inn, where the felon had
been spotted carrying several bundles and a camlet (a type of light
cloth) cloak, and ended beyond Inverurie. During the night-long chase
in which hunter and hunted crossed and recrossed the River Urie, they
exchanged pistol fire. At Kintore, the villain was finally overpowered by
a group of shoemakers while Geordie 'wus in at the death in a jiffey' and
'a pair o' mittens clappit on wi' little mair adee'. The man was sentenced
to death at the Circuit Court in Aberdeen but was reprieved and
banished from the country.

Geordie's duties included attending fairs and markets, a magnet for
all sorts of criminals, ranging from pickpockets to horse thieves. He and
a colleague would wear red coats, their badge of authority, discreetly
hidden under their jackets and never showed the scarlet unless there
was a hint of real trouble.

Geordie was handy with his fists in a tight corner but he could also
have given Sherlock Holmes a run for his money. In May 1837, he snared
a thief by footprints in the snow. He took an impression of the prints
on a piece of paper and compared them with the soles of boots worn
by a cattle-dealer at Huntly market. They matched and the thief was
transported for seven years. Two years earlier the 'prent o' the muckle

tackettie shee sole' in a Garioch blacksmith's yard helped nail Sawney Lindsay, an old smuggler – 'a coorse blackguard', according to Geordie – who had stolen bees. Geordie made the arrest in the small debt court in Aberdeen. With Lindsay 'fast by the heels', Geordie went round to the blackguard's 'hole o' a garret' in Gardiner's Lane. There he found the purloined bees, skeps and tubs of honey. Lindsay was jailed for a year and his woman, Isobel Milton, got six months for reset.

The Oldmeldrum sheriff and criminal officer made a number of unusual and daring arrests during a long and rousing career. In July 1838, he was enjoying himself right fine at the Reform Ball in Inverurie when, still in Highland dress, he was summoned to investigate a theft at Fyvie Castle. A butler, John Watson, had reported the theft of a quantity of linen and garments from his house at the castle. Geordie suspected Jane Ritchie, a former servant, who had sent a heavy leather-bound trunk by carrier to Oldmeldrum. He forced open the trunk and found Watson's sheets, towels, shirts and a clutch of pawnbroker's tickets. His next stop was pawnbroker William Ruddiman's shop in the Green in Aberdeen where he recovered more linen and other items stolen and pawned by Ritchie. Many items had belonged to fellow servants and were stolen by her in Aberdeen. Ritchie had never been suspected by any of her employers.

Geordie arrested Ritchie on her wedding day in Oldmeldrum, with her 'deckit up like a duchess'. The bride fainted, or pretended to faint, and one of the lassies at Barnett's Inn, where the wedding was scheduled to take place, ran and threw water in her face. Geordie, cried, '"Hoot, hoot," says I; tak' care an' nae weet 'er owre sair, for though I'm takin' 'er awa' fae the bridegreem, I'm takin' 'er to Aiberdeen in a braw cairriage.'

Geordie relieved the shoemaker bridegroom of 'a deev'lish ill wife' who gave birth to their son in jail in Aberdeen. 'It was a laddie, an' of coorse he grew up a freeman o' the toon, bein' born i' the jail.' His mother was tried at the Autumn Circuit and was transported for seven years.

In the spring of 1841, the intrepid officer disguised himself as an old woman to nab a poacher in the Earl of Kintore's woods at Ley Lodge. Geordie kept silent watch for four nights in a row before he finally arrested John Rose or Ross, a shoemaker, for snaring hares. He had deliberately cut the top off young trees to camouflage his traps. The cunning poacher probably smelt a rat and kept low. Geordie decided it was time for a change of plan and so disguised himself as an old gypsy woman. He borrowed a gown and round mutch from a Mrs Sim and, with a bundle over his shoulder, set off down a woodland path. Rose was surprised as he dropped the night's illegal catch into his sack. 'Lord preserve's!' shouted Rose. 'I thocht it was an aul' wife!' Replied his chortling captor, 'Ay, ay; an' sae – a gey queer aul' wife, tee. Hooever, pack ye up your traps an' come along, laddie.' Rose had sixty days in the Bridewell Prison in which to recover from the shock.

There was the time he tracked a pair of robbers, Jock and Geordie Williamson – 'roch oonchristian tykes' – and their gypsy clan from the Bridge of Alford to the Banffshire coast – at a sea cave at Troup Head, near Gardenstown. Geordie, backed up by a large group of farm servants who were armed with pitchforks and other weapons, headed for Troup Head.

> [We] slippit into the cave canny aneuch, an' got half-a-dizzen o' the tribe an' mair, wives an' bairns an' a', lyin' there deid drunk or sleepin', an' the sea washin' to the door o' their hoose. We hed them han'-cuff't ere they hardly got their een apen't, so there was nae difficulty in managing them.

Jock and Geordie, who had robbed George Scott, a travelling merchant from the Steps of Gilcomston in Aberdeen, were banished at the Spring Court of 1839.

Geordie's autobiography was based on his notebooks and no crime was too big or too small for him. While beadle at Oldmeldrum Church, he investigated the mystery of the vanishing collection! On three successive Sundays, the offering in the collection plate at the east door had been stolen even as the congregation began the first psalm. 'The minister an' the session wus in a maze aboot it,' recalled Geordie. Suspicion fell on James Crichton, an elder, whose job was to count the collection. But the beadle was determined to get to the bottom of the mystery. The following Sunday, he carried out the first part of his kirk duty before leaving with his hat in his hand. After walking towards the town, he doubled back, ducking behind dykes as he went. As he drew closer to the church, he crawled on hands and knees. As the first psalm rang out, a boy approached the plate at a crawl. He slipped the collection into his bonnet but, as he began to crawl away, Geordie leapt on to the back of the young rogue – the 'nickum Farquhar'. After the service, he told the minister, 'Jeems Crichton's an honest man.' Despite the minister's protests, Geordie marched the youngster off to jail.

In the early part of his career, he investigated a break-in at Sandy Bothwell's house in Kirk Street, Oldmeldrum, and the theft of a watch at George Hunter's farm at Mill of Easterton. The theft had been committed by William Simpson, one of Hunter's labourers, whom Geordie found hiding under the 'cauff (chaff) bed' at his home, with his 'wife an' 's family a' lyin' o' tap the bed abeen 'im. Of course he layna muckle langer there.' Simpson got seven years – but was 'deet afore his sentence was oot'.

Geordie Webster ranged far and wide to track down criminals. If not on foot, horseback or gig he would travel by stagecoach. *Tally ho, Earl of Fife* and *Lord Forbes* were some of the names of these coaches. In April 1835, he went in search of George Walker or Gray, a former guard on the Aberdeen-to-Elgin *Star* coach who had 'gane the black gate wi' drink' and stolen £91 from a Huntly merchant at Sangster's Inn at Newmachar. The trail ran cold. As Geordie pointed out, it could prove difficult catching a criminal who had a day or two's head start.

> Ye hed to set a' yer wits at wark than to get tracks o' him. It wasna – Warn Edinboro', Dundee or Glaisca by telegraph an' speer at the poleece richt an' left, 'Hae ye seen 'im? – five fit ten, licht hair, curled whiskers, an' a side-lang leuk – dressed in grey tweed fan last seen.' Na, na – jist a blin' glamp (a groping search in the dark); an' dash awa' upo' your ain skeel in search o' yer prisoner, man or 'oman. Letter vreetin' an' wytein' for days for an answer did ye little gweed.

By a stroke of luck, Geordie was returning from 'criminal bizness' in Liverpool the following spring when the *Union* coach stopped at Haddington. After a dram with the local police superintendent, he was invited to cast an eye over the prisoners in the lock-up – and in one cell he confronted the fugitive Walker, in jail for debt. Geordie took Walker to Aberdeen to be questioned on the theft charge. He returned with him to Edinburgh where he eventually faced a lengthier indictment of forgery, robbery or theft. He was tried at the next Circuit Court and banished.

In July 1843, he arrested a forger, James Duncan, at Portsoy and headed for Aberdeen on the top of the *Earl of Fife* coach. Duncan complained that his 'darbies' were chaffing his wrists so Geordie took off the cuffs. As the coach rattled at ten miles an hour through Rothie woods, the prisoner leapt from the coach, hurdled a dyke and vanished into the wood. Geordie set out in pursuit, followed by fellow passengers, a group of students, baying like a pack of foxhounds. Geordie ran Duncan to earth. At Oldmeldrum, the prisoner was put into leg irons for the last lap of the journey to Aberdeen. Geordie had covered no less than 122 miles on the case.

At the end of the previous year, he had gone in search of a man called Nicol – 'to Edinburgh, to Glasgow, to Greenock an' back, pairt railway, pairt coach, occupied one week, 400 miles in all'. Nicol gave him the slip and was outlawed at the next Circuit Court.

Geordie Webster risked life and limb. In 1836, he was badly hurt while making a difficult arrest at a slate quarry at Tillymorgan. Murdoch Finlayson, a 'great robust and young deevle', hurled him down a slate-strewn slope when he tried to apprehend him for a serious assault at a local fair. Despite a serious head injury, he managed to overpower the man with the help of some quarrymen and rope him to a cart. In court next day, Sheriff Watson eyed the arresting officer's bandaged head and remarked he had obviously been 'at the wars'. Geordie replied, 'Oh, yes, sir. I've been at the wars, an' bear the marks upo' me.'

Oldmeldrum's criminal officer of the 'old school' damaged his ribs when caught up in an 'unholy row' at Culsalmond old parish church, now an empty shell. It was the early days of the Disruption, when 451 ministers of the Church of Scotland and almost a third of its membership left the established church, on the principle of spiritual independence from the state, to form the Free Kirk. At stake was the right of a congregation to 'call' its own minister without accepting one through patronage. On a cold, stormy day in October 1841, a crowd of 2,000 and more besieged the kirk to prevent the new minister being 'settled' and a minister from Inverurie was chased through a turnip field. Geordie was in the thick of things, of course, along with other sheriff's officers and the police, and his involvement was described by William Alexander in his classic Doric novel, *Johnny Gibb of Gushetneuk*, first published in 1891. In his own account of the riot, Geordie wrote:

> But a' the officers an' police there cudna stem ae grain; an' naitrally steed a peer chance, for I was yarkit in aside the door and knockit doon. An' I suppose fifty o' them gaed richt owre me wi' their feet, the haethens.

The mob smashed all the windows in the kirk and the new minister, Rev. William Middleton, was inducted in the manse. Geordie suffered broken ribs at the hands of the 'roch scoonrels' and was carried to the manse and put to bed. That night, he went home in Sheriff Murray's carriage to recuperate – with pay.

Geordie religiously noted his arrests and expenses in his little 'beuks'. His pawky humour is apparent from the following extracts.

> The simmer o' 1841 was occupiet wi' fat ye mith ca' miscellaneous cases … July 1st, apprenhendin' ane James Wishart for forgery; syne at the middle o' the same month awa to Laurencekirk, Brechin, Arbroath, Dundee an' Glasgow aifter anither forger; an' on the 24th doon to Banff for George Chalmers, 't hed been flunky at Meldrum Hoose. Oh, he was chairg't wi' theft, an' got sixty days in jail. On August 10th, apprenhendin' Alexander Munro, carter, of Cottown, for assault on Charles McCrae; that was Charles the vintner in Meldrum, ye ken. He kicket up a great row, an' brak Charles' windows an' the vera door, the great haethen. He was in drink of coorse; but he got sixty days to sober upon 't ony wye. On the 22nd October, I was o' the hunt to Stanehive (Stonehaven), the fisherton o' Downies, an' Stripeside, Fetteresso, aifter Catherine Thain, alias Ann Robertson, an' I got her in Widow Falconer's there. It was a case of theft at Forres, an' she got thirty days.

At the beginning of November 1841, Geordie arrested Joseph Tohetto for breaking into a wright's shop and stealing tools. The culprit had buried the tools in fields and, according to his captor, was 'given sixty days private lodgin's in Aberdeen'. In a case of malicious mischief near Turriff, three farm servants, Alexander Forbes, Alexander Grant and James Grieve, tore down hayricks belonging to Adam Chapman, a crofter at Redhill of Auchterless, and also trussed up the poor man with rope.

'Arcadian innocence an' simplicity, said ye, Sir?' Geordie asked his readers. 'I ken naething about Arcadian nor Kirkcaldian innocence; but that was a piece o' curs't mischief ony wye; an' they paid for 't wi' sixty days i' the jail, an' sair't them right tee, I tell ye!'

Geordie wrote somewhat scornfully of the Aberdeen County Constabulary of 1880:

> Fat? There's nae ae vagabon' the day, I tell ye, faur there was a dizzeen – ay a score – fan I began; and ye've seyventy or auchty police i' the Coonty stappin' roon' like as mony mull horse, ilka ane on's beat deein' fat ae man – that's mysel' an' nae ither – hed to dee maist single han' it.

Geordie, a remarkable, if pompous character, had dealings with equally colourful folk on his travels. There was James Lamb, an itinerant tailor in Muckle Wartle, who was the victim of a theft at Wartle market in 1837. A 'coorse randie', Jane Greig or Stratton, lifted his watch and eighteen shillings in silver. The woman, who had a criminal record, was nabbed by Geordie and given seven years' banishment at the Autumn Circuit in Aberdeen. Jeems, it seems, was 'an aul' creatur wi' blue knee-breeks an' ribbet hose, an' a red nightcap on 's heid'. It was said Jeems was a superstitious soul and frightened of 'bogles and boodies'. On a dark night, he would pluck up courage by holding up his scissors in front of him while 'clip clippin' awa' at naething ava' ', as he hurried along a road.

Geordie thought himself a bit of a philosopher. In 1839, he took the road to Dundee and Perth in search of a bigamist, John Grub, a plasterer, who had married Mary Leslie a few months after marrying Margaret Littlejohn in the parish of Tarves during the harvest time of 1838. In his opinion, they were both respectable lassies and far too good for Grub. 'But it's won'erfu' fat wye respectable women'll some-times mae only tak' up wi' the greatest rag in creation, but stick till 'im 's gin he war an angel of licht; aifter he's deen things 'at the vera deil wud think shame to be liken't till.' Grub was sentenced to a year's imprisonment at the Spring Circuit. Mary was the cook at General Gordon's when Geordie was a groom there.

Geordie's services would seem to have been indispensable, even with the inauguration of the new police force. Fiscal Simpson was heard to say he would rather lose his horse and carriage than lose Oldmeldrum's criminal officer!

Eight years before the 'pitifu' ' story of John Booth, the last man to be publicly hanged in Aberdeen, the hand that gripped seven murderers reached out for James Robb, the Auchterless murderer and rapist, whose victim was Mary Smith, a quiet, sixty-two-year-old spinster who lived alone in her cottage at Redhill.

Robb, a twenty-two-year-old labourer at the Tillymorgan slate quarry, committed the crime after forcing entry into Mary's one-roomed home – 'a peer solitary kin' o' hut' is how Geordie described it – by way of the chimney. On the night of 9 April 1849, Robb left Badenscoth Fair the worse of drink, vowing that he was determined to gratify his passion on somebody before he slept. Mary was aware of Robb's violent reputation and had remarked casually to someone that she was 'not afraid of anybody, except that lad Jamie Robb'. Unfortunately, Robb had to pass her house on the road home to Fisherford. Next morning, neighbours, who were concerned that there was no sign of Mary about her place, entered the cottage and found her body. The bed was broken and bed-clothes crumpled. Propped against the exterior wall of the house was a distinctive walking stick, which belonged to her killer.

The police arrested Robb who was taken before Mr Barclay, a justice of the peace, at Knockleith. After an examination of sorts, Barclay allowed the chief suspect to go. James Strachan, the innkeeper at Badenscoth, passed word of the crime and Robb's release to Geordie Webster but it was twelve hours before the messenger, Jock McCrae, delivered it. A fuming Geordie threatened McCrae with jail for his tardiness before they both set off by carriage for Badenscoth as if the Devil was after them. At crossroads outside Inverurie, a frantic Geordie mistook an approaching carriage as the sheriff's. He feared he would lose face if the sheriff and fiscal reached the murder scene before him so he ordered his driver to hold on full gallop and not allow the other vehicle to pass. He breathed more easily when the carriage turned off the road.

Geordie dragged the dumbfounded Robb from his bed in his father's house and, pointing at his soot-smeared corduroy trousers, demanded, 'You stupid idiot, fat d'ye mean by that?' Geordie arrested Robb on the spot and that night they lodged at the inn at Badenscoth and downed punch in a room before a roaring fire. While McCrae kept watch at the bedside, the intrepid Geordie catnapped while chained to Robb, who was at his side in leg irons. In the course of that extraordinary night, Robb admitted he had entered Mary Smith's house by the chimney but denied murder. He claimed he had wanted a light for his pipe (it transpired he had asked admittance upon pretence of getting a light but had been refused). The fiscal turned up next morning with the sheriff and was not too pleased to hear that his officer had been sleeping alongside a murderer.

Robb was then taken to Mary Smith's cottage where he was confronted with her body. Two important clues implicated Robb. Ironically for Robb, the fireplace was fitted with a 'hinging lum' – a square wooden canopy, about five feet high by two and a half feet wide, placed about eight feet above the hearth. Streaks consistent with marks left by corduroy trousers of the kind Robb was wearing could be seen in the chimney's soot. A distinctive metal button on Robb's velvet coat had been broken as he overpowered his victim. The missing piece was found in a 'lirk' (fold or crease) of a sheet in Mary's bed.

By the time Geordie reached Aberdeen, it was getting late. The governor of the prison was attending a meeting out of town, meaning he was unable to hand over his prisoner. Geordie was 'terrified' to leave Robb out of his sight till properly secured so he took him along to Mrs McHardy's lodgings in the Adelphi 'an' got redd o' him neist mornin', poor Devil'.

The trial at the Autumn Circuit Court in Aberdeen was held behind closed doors. Robb denied the charge of murder and 'raptus'. After a thirty-five-minute adjournment, the jury returned a verdict of guilty but recommended mercy as they thought he had no intention of committing murder. Mr Shand, defending, submitted that, since the jury had expressly ruled out intent to murder, the sentence should not reflect that crime but his objection was overruled.

In his published diaries, Lord Cockburn, who was one of the judges, revealed he had no sympathy for the condemned man:

> It is difficult to drive the horrors of that scene out of one's imagination. The solitary old woman in the solitary house, the descent through the chimney, the beastly attack, the death struggle – all that was going on within this lonely room, amidst silent fields, and under a still, dark sky.

It is a fragment of hell, which it is both difficult to endure and to quit. Yet a jury, though clear of both crimes, recommended the brute to mercy! because he did not intend to commit the murder! Neither does the highwayman, who only means to wound, in order to get the purse, but kills.

Cockburn revealed that, within a few hours of being convicted, Robb had confessed and explained that the poor woman had died in his very grip. The cause of death, according to the doctors, said Cockburn, was 'an incipient disease of the heart'.

Calcraft made his first appearance in Aberdeen to hang Robb on 16 October 1849.

In the twilight of his life, Geordie Webster said of his long and eventful career, 'It was all done in the public interest, and for the public good; a terror to evildoers, and a protection to such as do well.' He died on 1 March 1883, aged eighty-three. He is buried in Meldrum Parish Church where, in 1838, he nabbed the 'nickum Farquhar', who filched the kirk offering. A granite slab marks the resting place of Geordie, his wife Margaret Rae, who predeceased him by almost four years, and four of their children, three of whom died in childhood.

Mary Webster, who died in May 1920, was the grandmother of the late Sime Halliday. When I spoke to him in his native Meldrum some years ago, he was one of Geordie's oldest surviving descendants. As a schoolboy, he had been unaware of his famous ancestor's exploits until one day he was in the town library when the local chemist handed him a slim, red-bound volume. 'Here, laddie', he said, 'take this book, you'll find it an interesting read.' It was Geordie Webster's self-published autobiography.

17

REST WITHOUT PEACE

The storm had raged for two nights but, by the morning of Thursday 1 December 1881, the wind had dropped to a low moan. The rain had ceased beating on the windows of Dunecht House and on the black skeletal trees, sodden lawns, shrubbery and swollen lakes of the sprawling Aberdeenshire estate.

The Victorian mansion loomed darkly above estate labourer William Hadden as he hurried to work. He rounded a corner of the Gothic chapel, adjoining the grey granite house, and stopped in his tracks. The iron railing which enclosed the vault below had been damaged. A layer of soil had been shovelled off the flagstones and a heavy granite block, measuring six feet by four feet, which had sealed the vault, was propped open by pieces of wood. Nearby lay two shovels and a pickaxe. Hadden believed his workmates, who had finished at five o'clock the previous evening, were responsible.

The estate commissioner, William Yeats, an Aberdeen advocate was contacted by telegram and he hurried to Dunecht, twelve miles away, accompanied by Inspector George Cran of Aberdeen County Constabulary. They were joined by Constable John Robb, the policeman from nearby Echt, and, by afternoon, they stood at the top of the short flight of steps which dropped into the dark crypt below.

The new mausoleum under the Gothic chapel, Dunecht House's most stunning feature, had space for sixty-four coffins arranged in tiers but it contained only one body, that of Alexander William Lindsay, born in 1812, who had succeeded to the title of 25th Earl of Crawford and 8th Earl of Balcarres in 1869.

Because of ill health, the Earl of Crawford, a noted astronomer, theologian, antiquarian and genealogist, had wintered in Egypt and Italy. Despite having escaped the harshness of the Scottish winter, on 13 December 1880, he died in Florence. His body was embalmed and then sealed inside three coffins. The inner coffin, the deceased's casket, was made of soft Italian wood. The middle one was lead and the outer one was made of highly polished, carved oak and was mounted with ornate silver. The coffins were then deposited within a huge walnut shell bearing a carving of a cross in high relief. The total weight was almost half a ton.

The late earl might have expected to be buried in the old vault beneath the Lindsay family chapel at Wigan Parish Church in Lancashire. But the vault was full so it was decided the he would be interred in the Gothic chapel at Dunecht House. His body was transported across the Alps in the company of a faithful retainer, before being lashed to the deck of a chartered steamer for the Channel crossing from France. At Aberdeen, the outer shell had to be removed before it could be safely transported by road to Dunecht. During the body's journey north, Scotland was swept by a violent snowstorm and the hearse was trapped for several days in drifts on the journey back to Aberdeen.

The white-marbled mortuary chapel had not been consecrated at the time of the earl's death so the Episcopal Bishop of Aberdeen performed the rite before interment on 29 December 1880. The heavy outer shell was deposited in the vault beside the huge sarcophagus, which was manhandled into place by eight men. Four heavy slabs of Caithness granite were laid across the flight of eight steps leading from the entrance of the tomb to the floor of the crypt. Finally, the heavy granite block sealed the entrance.

Now, on that cold afternoon on the first day of December in 1881, it was believed that no one else had set foot in the vault since the interment but Inspector Cran, lighted candle in hand, got a nasty shock when he descended into the crypt. He shouted on Robb and Yeats to follow. The tools that lay at the entrance of the tomb belonged to labourers carrying out building work and had been left the previous night. On the stairs, they almost fell over three iron bars and two planks but they were unprepared for the horrifying sight of the desecrated tomb. Its floor was strewn with planks and sawdust, which emitted a strong scent, and three coffins, which had been dumped on their side and rifled.

The Earl of Crawford's body was missing!

The lids of the two wooden coffins had been carefully unscrewed while the leaden shell had been sawn open from corner to corner, envelope fashion, and the four corners forced back. The sawdust, it was noted, was mildewed and the leaden shell had turned rusty where it had been hacked open. This led the police to the realisation that some considerable time had elapsed since the daring theft. Inspector Cran had barely recovered from the grim discovery when he was handed another shock. Yeats had been told of the theft three months earlier!

He showed the policeman an anonymous letter he had received on 8 September. It bore an Aberdeen postmark and read:

> Sir, The remains of the late Earl of Crawford are not beneath the chaple (sic) at Dunecht as you believe, but were removed hence last spring, and the smell of decayed flowers, ascending from the vault since that time will, on investigation, be found to proceed from another cause than flowers. NABOB.

Yeats had discussed the letter with the builder of the vault and decided it was a tasteless hoax. But he had the good sense not to destroy it. Other pieces of the jigsaw fell into place. The lawyer told Cran that, at the end of May, he had received reports of a strong odour wafting up from the vault. The housekeeper who had passed the vault on her way to church described it as 'pleasantly aromatic'. Next day, the gardener had also noticed the odour, which he blamed on decaying wreaths left in the crypt, as outlined by 'NABOB'. A crack between the flagstones was thought to have been caused by frost and was repaired with lime and cement. The vault was not reopened and instead the area was covered with soil, sown with grass and the iron railing erected.

Detectives reasoned that, when the late earl's family took no action on receiving the letter, someone had returned to desecrate the vault again so that the crime would be discovered. The nation was outraged. It stirred memories of the bodysnatchers. Queen Victoria sent a message of sympathy to the new peer and his family. The Aberdeen *Evening Express* commented:

Body-lifting, though common enough in this as in other districts some fifty years ago, is a crime now almost unknown: and the horror raised by this sacrilegious act is, if anything, deepened by the skill, patience and masterly villainy that seems to have been brought to bear in its conception and execution.

The crime was depicted in *The Illustrated London News*, the world-famous panoramic journal.

More than 100 police and estate workers scoured the seventy-acre Dunecht policies and surrounding countryside and a guard was mounted on the big house. Searchers were hampered by a severe snowstorm.

Wild rumours and theories about the bodysnatching circulated in north-east Scotland. It was whispered that the earl's body was stolen in Florence to learn the secrets of embalming; that the family themselves were behind the theft so as to give them an excuse to sell their Scottish estate; that revenge was the motive; that the dark deed had been the work of Italian decorators working on the Dunecht chapel and the corpse had been shipped back to Florence. Even a newspaper reporter was suspected!

Police suspected that someone with inside knowledge of the Dunecht estate was to blame. When further letters arrived, threatening to destroy the earl's body unless £6,000 was paid to the letter writer, the mysterious 'NABOB' was the prime suspect. But more than one person, probably a gang, was behind the crime. It was beyond belief that someone could have single-handedly uprooted the sarcophagus from its niche in the vault.

Attempts were made to contact the anonymous letter writer, with appeals in the local press pleading, 'Nabob. Please communicate at once.'

A further appeal, sweetened with a reward of £50 for more information, saw this inexpertly penned letter to the family's London solicitor:

Sir, the late Earl of Crawford. The body is still in Aberdeenshire, and I can put you in possession of the same as soon as you bring one or more of the desperados who stole it to justice so that I may know with whom I have to deal. I have no wish to be assinated by rusarectionests, nor suspected by the public of being an accomplice in such dastardly work, which I most assuredly would be unless the guilty party are brought to justice. Had Mr Yeats acted on the hint I gave him last Sept., he might have found the remains as though by axeand and was hunted up the robers at Isure, but the chance is lost, so I hope you will find your men and make it safe and prudent for me to find what you want. P.S. – Should they find out thad an outsider knows their secret it may be removed to another place. NABOB.

The body had not been lifted for medical research but for financial gain. Similar outrages had been perpetrated elsewhere. In 1876, a gang of American counterfeiters was surprised in the act of stealing President Lincoln's body in Washington. They had hoped to return the body in exchange for master engraver Ben Boyd, who was in jail. Two years later, the corpse of New York millionaire merchant, Mr T. A. Stewart, was stolen but, despite his widow's offer to pay the ransom, it was never recovered.

On the advice of the Home Secretary, the deceased earl's family refused to offer a reward for the recovery of the body. Instead, a £600 reward (£500 from the family and £100 from the government) and a free pardon to anyone involved, other than the actual perpetrator, were offered for information leading to the arrest of the culprit.

Public interest in the Dunecht mystery never flagged – there was always something new to keep their curiosity aroused. A bloodhound called 'Morgan' provided a farcical diversion when his trainer, a Mr Spencer of Wigan, brought him north. Morgan, described by the press as the 'famous sleuth hound', had earned his reputation in Blackburn, Lancashire, in March 1876, when he found the remains of seven-year-old Emily Mary Holland and helped put the hangman's noose around the neck of her murderer, William Fish (29), a barber. Mr Spencer boasted of his dog's exploits in capturing two burglars. 'We started at seven, and by half-past eleven the thieves had got three months apiece.' But Morgan failed to perform in Dunecht Woods. At the curt command of 'Seek, dead!', the 'sagacious' hound, which had been given a whiff of the sawdust that had been used in packing the earl's body, bounded after rabbits. A hoar frost was also hindrance. Undeterred, the public queued on Hogmanay to pay the sixpence (2.5p) admission to see 'the famous Morgan' at the annual Aberdeen Dog Show in Woolmanhill Hall.

Amateur crime-busters and local clairvoyants got in on the act, much to the annoyance of the police, but there was still no trace of the body. Peter Castle, an Aberdeen wine merchant, described himself as an 'amateur detective'. He took an obsessive interest in the case and actually got himself hired by the new earl. On one occasion, Castle was on a train from Aberdeen to Edinburgh when he noticed 'the suspicious proceedings of two foreign-looking individuals who were in the train, and who had along with them a peculiarly shaped box'. No doubt he believed the late earl was in the box but nothing more was heard of this strange encounter.

Castle failed to persuade a Professor Coates, who had been lecturing on 'Mesmerism and Phrenology' in Aberdeen, to help solve the Dunecht mystery but later enlisted the help of local clairvoyant Donald Christie, who claimed the elusive corpse was hidden in St Margaret's Episcopal Church in the city's Gallowgate. Christie's strange behaviour alarmed the sisters and police were called to eject him. The public ridiculed Christie, nicknaming him, 'The Dunecht Dreamer'. They would also lose patience with Castle.

In February 1882 the police caused a sensation when they arrested two men in connection with the theft. They were named as Thomas Kirkwood, a joiner on the Dunecht Estate, and John Philip, an Aberdeen shoemaker, who had formerly been a drill instructor of the Echt Volunteers. Kirkwood had given himself up in London when he heard police were looking for him. Philip was suspected of being 'NABOB'. The police had acted on a tip-off from a member of the public. His name, Peter Castle. But after a few days in custody the men were released.

The mystery took a dramatic turn on Tuesday 18 July 1882, when the body of the late Earl of Crawford was found wrapped in blankets and buried in a shallow grave, about 500 yards from his favourite study at Dunecht House. It was found after an eight-hour search in the course of an old ditch, close by a gravel pit, by police and gamekeepers using iron probes. The police had acted on a tip-off from Aberdeen game dealer George Machray. On the day the body was recovered, police announced the arrest of the bearded Charles Soutar (42), a mole- and rat-catcher, who lived in Aberdeen. Machray had been a gamekeeper at Ury, Stonehaven, when Soutar worked there are as a rat-catcher. Machray had gone to the police following meetings with Soutar who hinted at having inside knowledge of the crime.

At one meeting in an Aberdeen pub, Soutar asked Machray to act as a go-between with the late earl's agent so that he 'could tell where the body was on two conditions, namely they would find out the persons who took the body, and give protection to him'.

On the day of his arrest Soutar, of Donald's Court, Schoolhill, was judicially examined by Sheriff Comrie Thomson in Aberdeen and admitted he had written the 'NABOB' letters. On being asked, 'What do you know of the removal of the late Earl of Crawford's body?' Soutar revealed an astonishing tale. He claimed that, while poaching in Crow Wood, near Dunecht House, late one night in late April or early May 1881, he was ambushed by two men. He made a run for it but was tripped up and pinned to the ground. His attackers, 'young-like chaps, of middle size', had their faces blackened. They spoke with Aberdeenshire accents and seemed 'common'. As he lay sprawled on the ground, they were joined by two masked accomplices. The new arrivals were of a different stamp. They appeared to be 'gentlemen' and spoke like educated men. Soutar claimed one of the men threatened him with a revolver at his breast. He said to his companion, 'Remove your arm and I will settle him.' The other replied, 'It's all right. It's the rat-catcher. He's poaching.'

Soutar was told if he had been a spy he would have been shot, with the added threat, 'Remember what I am going to tell you; you're known to our party, and if you breathe a syllable of what you have seen, I will have your life if you're on the face of the earth.' He was released but, at daybreak, he returned to the spot and found a man's body wrapped in a blanket. He thought he had stumbled upon a murder victim. The corpse smelled of benzoline and he believed efforts had been made to destroy it. Soutar refused to take police to the spot remarking, 'I'll rather wait until you get them that took the body; it will be safer for me.'

Soutar's strange tale was read out by the prosecution at his trial in the High Court in Edinburgh on Monday 23 October 1882, when he was accused of violating the sepulchres of the dead and of the raising and carrying away of dead bodies out of their graves.

No witnesses were cited for the defence and there was little or no cross-examination by Soutar's counsel but the Dean of Faculty did make one point – the crime could not have been committed by Soutar alone and, therefore, the mystery was only half-solved. The Crown pinpointed 27 or 28 May 1881 as the date of the outrage, as any earlier attempt would have been hampered because of the severe winter of 1880–81. So, if that had been the case, the body would have lain hidden for fourteen months.

Soutar was spotted by several witnesses in the vicinity of Dunecht House, where he had worked for five or six years before being sacked for poaching three years before the Earl of Crawford died. Two men, who were arrested during the police investigation but later freed, gave evidence for the prosecution. They were Philip, the Echt shoemaker, and James Collier (37), a Glasgow tram driver and former Echt sawyer, who recognised the prisoner on the Cluny coach from Aberdeen on 17 May 1881. He knew Soutar had recently been released from jail (in 1878, Soutar was imprisoned for eighteen months for his involvement in a poaching incident which resulted in the death of a police sergeant). Mrs Leith, the keeper of the inn at Waterton of Echt, close to Dunecht House, saw Soutar get off the coach and walk towards Echt. Where he went, what he did and who else he met were unknown.

In his charge to the jury at the end of the two-day trial, Lord Craighill, the presiding judge, agreed that it was:

> perfectly impossible that one man alone could accomplish what had been done; probably more than two were concerned. The vault was opened and closed the same night without suspicion being aroused, and not only strength but skill was employed in the perpetration of this offence.

He went on:

> The body was removed, the grave was dug, and all traces of these operations were obliterated. Probably these things were not all done on a single night, and certainly one man could not have done them; there must have been others. The guilt of the prisoner, however, if he were concerned, was in law the same as if he had been the sole offender.

Soutar was found guilty and sentenced to five years' penal servitude.

Machray, Philip and Collier claimed the £600 reward offered for information leading to Soutar's capture. But, in 1883, Sheriff Guthrie

Smith of Aberdeen awarded half the reward to Machray because he considered Soutar had not been acting alone. Philip sued the earl's London solicitor for slander. The case was settled out of court. Collier, who later turned his hand to journalism, bitterly criticised the bumbling Peter Castle in a pamphlet, claiming that it was his 'meddling' which led to the arrest of Philip and Kirkwood. Castle became a figure of ridicule in Aberdeen and his effigy was burned on April Fool's Day 1882. He later became bankrupt and was forced to leave Scotland for Liverpool.

On his release in 1887, Soutar admitted writing the 'NABOB' letters but denied stealing the body. He identified the real criminals but their names were not revealed by the press. One of his visitors to the jail was a member of the Scottish aristocracy, the Earl of Fife, but the reason for his visit was not revealed. He was probably a friend of the Lindsay family.

The Earl of Crawford's body was finally interred in the Lindsay family crypt at Wigan after the town council gave special permission for the old vault to be reopened after a quarter of a century.

The Dowager, Lady Crawford, erected a small granite cross at the place where her husband's body was found. The inscription records the theft and adds:

> He shall give his angels charge over thee
> He that keepeth thee will not slumber

The audacious crime led to the estate being advertised for sale in 1886. It was sold in 1900 to A. C. Pirie of Craibstone and, in 1908, it was purchased by Weetman Pearson, First Viscount Cowdray, whose worldwide engineering feats involved building canals, railways, harbours and tunnels, notably the Hudson and East River tunnels in New York. His biographer has left an intriguing footnote to the outrage when he wrote, 'Whatever spell the superstitious may have supposed to have been cast on the place by this incident was quickly broken by the cheerful Cowdray touch.'

Today the crypt at Dunecht House serves as a double garage but you can still see traces of the Victorian catacombs. The earl's coffin, a 'production' during the trial, was deposited in the vaults of old Parliament House in Edinburgh, now the Court of Session.

18

'NELLFIELD PIES!'

Oh, the horror! Could the stories be true? Rumours were going about that in order to make room for fresh interments, grave-diggers had deliberately exhumed corpses and the decaying remains they unearthed were then buried under the footpaths at Nellfield Cemetery. It was even said that the bodies of children and their coffins were burned in a furnace!

At six o'clock on the morning of Tuesday 6 June 1899, official excavations to find the truth began at the high-walled graveyard in the west end of Aberdeen. The ghoulish revelations of the four-day search sent shock waves through Victorian Britain.

The first hint of the 'Nellfield Cemetery Scandals' was given at the city's Sheriff Court in May, when a civil action was brought against the cemetery owners, the Aberdeen Baker Incorporation, alleging interference with a lair owned by the Harvey family of Aberdeen. Revelations by witnesses to further cases of desecration of graves alerted the police and the public to the horrors to come.

At the centre of the scandal was William Coutts, the cemetery superintendent. After a criminal investigation, he was under arrest when the excavations began on that bright, warm morning. Onlookers, informed of the starting time of the search by the previous night's *Evening Express*, had already gathered opposite the cemetery's main gate in Great Western Road. In the days to come, the police would erect wooden screens in an effort to deter the curious.

Police stood guard as Mr T. Maclennan, the procurator-fiscal depute, arrived, followed by Dr Matthew Hay, medical officer of health, James McDonald, the deacon of the Baker Incorporation, John Warrack, the cemetery factor, and two solicitors, one of whom was Coutts's agent. A police inspector arrived by horse-drawn cab with a pile of bulky ledgers connected with burials. Two detectives prepared to take notes as council workmen rolled up their sleeves. Picks and shovels were the order of the day but some clutched iron rods to establish the depth of the burials.

It was just as well that Coutts was being held in Craiginches Prison for each shovelful during the long and harrowing search unearthed a fresh horror. The exhumation teams found un-coffined corpses, human skulls and bones crammed below the paths. Gravediggers broke up the coffins in their tool house, the shed where they kept their tools, and then burned the bits in a furnace close by the cemetery. A nearby pit was found to contain four hundred coffin handles, coffin nameplates and ashes. Some bodies had been doubled up and buried two feet below the surface and the bodies of two women had been crushed into one coffin. In one lair opposite the Great Western Place gate, there had been twenty-nine burials inside three months, with the bodies being disinterred immediately after and thrown into other pits. Checks of ledgers listing burials revealed that bodies had been lifted without the knowledge of relatives and re-interred elsewhere in the cemetery.

The newspaper stories were graphic and stomach-churning and the public came to see for themselves. An *Aberdeen Journal* reporter noted that a row of eight coffins was in full view of passengers on the top deck of tramcars in Great Western Road. Urchins viewed proceedings from behind chimney pots while message boys turned their barrows, piled high with boxes and parcels, into makeshift grandstands. Although the cemetery was closed to the public, funerals went ahead as planned. An intrepid *Journal* reporter outwitted police by posing as a mourner to get his story.

The press had a field day, with the *Journal* and the *Evening Express* selling thousands of extra copies. The 'Nellfield Cemetery Scandals' shocked the whole nation. *The Pall Mall Gazette* reported that the 'body-snatching of an earlier day was scarcely equal to this'. *The News of the World* observed:

> The reports from Aberdeen rival the stories of Burke and Hare in gruesomeness and horror. They indicate that no respect whatsoever has been paid to the sanctity of the tomb. There is too much reason to fear

that Aberdeen is not the only centre where such ghoulish performances take place, and the investigations may tend to reveal similar scandals in other places.

Questions about the affair were raised in Parliament.

In Aberdeen, Warrack, the cemetery factor, was hounded by stick-wielding youths when he left the cemetery on the Friday, the second last day of the excavations. They screamed, 'Burn the bodies!' and 'Nellfield scoundrel!' as he fled on foot to his baker's shop in Chapel Street. Two policemen, one of whom hitched a ride on a tramcar, sped to his rescue. When the mob threatened to get out of hand, reinforcements were summoned by telephone and the crowd eventually dispersed. The public boycotted Warrack's shop and he complained that his van boys were returning with unsold bread because customers' children refused to eat it.

When Coutts was eventually allowed bail by the court, his transport was dogged by a mob crying, 'Nellfield pies!' – which gives more than a hint of the sort of rumours sweeping the Granite City. Even so, Coutts was reported to be remarkably well and in good spirits when reunited with his family at their home in Ferryhill Terrace. His job, which brought a salary of £70 a year and a free house, had been advertised and was expected to be filled soon. There would be sixty applicants from all over the country.

The trial of William Coutts opened at the High Court of Justiciary in Aberdeen on Wednesday 6 September 1899. There was a moment of light relief at the start when Coutts was summoned to the dock and a juryman with the same name answered. Lord McLaren was the judge. The prosecution was led by James A. Fleming, the advocate depute, and the defence counsel was J. Crabb Watt, advocate, of Edinburgh. Coutts, who wore a navy blue suit, pleaded not guilty to seven charges on the indictment – six of violating sepulchres and one of perjury, arising from the Harvey civil action.

The grave-diggers at Nellfield, where interments were as high as eight a day, admitted carrying out their sickening practices on the superintendent's orders and described how they broke up corpses with shovels and 'coupit' the body parts from a barrow into a pit, or dragged them along the ground. Coffins, and not corpses, were burned. One grave-digger, John Hay junior, denied having a grudge against Coutts.

He also denied informing lair-holders of the desecration of graves and taking an active part in getting up the Harvey case against the Aberdeen Baker Incorporation.

In the course of the trial, the reason behind the desecration became clear. The removal of coffins from certain lairs created room for new burials, which meant more income. It also saved the workmen back-breaking toil as it meant less earth had to be carted off than if the whole coffin had been buried. But Coutts had no sordid personal motive in his grim work – nor had he made any personal monetary profit. His employers would have welcomed the extra revenue, of course, but they were kept in the dark about his gruesome methods.

Prisoners had recently been allowed to be examined on their own behalf but Coutts did not go into the box on the fourth and final day. Instead, his counsel tendered pleas of guilty to two of the charges of violating sepulchres and this was accepted by the advocate depute. Mr Watt, defending, described Coutts as honest, respectable and obliging. He said he had received little instruction in running the cemetery, which he had joined as a gardener. He had no personal motive and, in fact, he really did not believe he was committing a crime.

In his address to the jury, Lord McLaren said the bodies had been 'taken out and disposed of with a callous brutality which sent a shiver through the frame of every person present'. His Lordship went on:

> I hope that the exposure of the conduct of the internments in this cemetery, so revolting in its details and shocking to the natural feelings – not only of the relatives of those who are removed, but of many who may fear that their dead might be treated in the same way – will probably prove an effective safeguard against the possibility of such practices continuing in any cemetery in Scotland. I may perhaps add that, should anything of this kind again take place, the attention of the authorities will now be directed to these matters, and no person accused can plead ignorance of the law.

He then directed the jury to find Coutts guilty of the two charges of violating sepulchres and not guilty of the other charges. The jury agreed.

Lord McLaren, in passing sentence, told Coutts:

I take into account, in considering the punishment, that, in the first place, it must be a substantial punishment, in order to satisfy the ends of justice. It is not of the most severe character, because this is not a case of raising bodies for sale, which would be theft: neither was it done for the purpose of exhorting money by working upon the feelings of relatives. It was a case of breach of trust to the relatives who paid for these internments. In such circumstances, your acts constituted, by the law of Scotland, a violation of sepulchres. I am also willing – very willing – to give what weight I can to the points so well submitted and brought out by your counsel that this is the first case in which it has been found necessary to take action against any cemetery officials for a series of desecrations, and, therefore, though you must know that your conduct amounted to a moral offence, you may not have been fully aware of the criminal responsibility that resulted from your acts. In the circumstances, I feel warranted in limiting the sentence to a period of six months' imprisonment.

The *Evening Express* broke the news within minutes of receiving the verdict from their court reporter. A special edition was hawked around the streets by an 'army of newsboys' and every available horse-drawn cab was snapped up to circulate the paper throughout the city. In Aberdeen the Boer War had been reduced to a sideshow.

As the prisoner was conveyed by 'Black Maria' from the courthouse to Craiginches, public opinion was unequivocal – Coutts had got off lightly. The London press felt the nightmare at Nellfield had strengthened the case for cremation of the dead.

Days later Barnum and Bailey's three-ringed circus, *The Greatest Show on Earth*, hit town. The great parade of exotic performers, horses, elephants, camels, lions, tigers, leopards, panthers, hyenas, wolves and bears rolled through the streets which were lined with thousands of spectators. The parade left the showground at Central Park, Kittybrewster, moving at the leisurely pace of three miles an hour. Its route, which took three hours to travel, was along George Street, Hutcheon Street, Mount Street, Rosemount Place, Beechgrove Terrace, Fountainhall Road, Queen's Cross and Union Street. They then turned back, via King Street, and arrived at the showground where they put on sell-out shows. It was just the boost the city needed.

LAST WORDS

In May 1865, George Stephen, the Thainstone axe murderer, was saved from the hangman's rope four days before Calcraft was due to execute him in Aberdeen. When the Lord Provost, accompanied by magistrates and prison officials, arrived at the jail to break the good news, Stephen betrayed no emotion. In reply to a question, as to whether he knew what it all meant, a stony-faced Stephen replied, 'Ou, aye; jist a whilie langer to live!'

In 1893, farm worker Robert Smith was locked up in Peterhead Prison for life after being found guilty of culpable homicide. He was lucky to escape the gallows as he had caused the death of a fellow workman and fatally injured another man on a farm near Stonehaven. He was equally ungrateful when told a petition might be organised to have him released. 'Dae nae such thing,' he fumed. 'I was niver sae happy and comfortable a' my life. The meat is guid and aye sure, and ye ha'e a roof abeen your heid. It's far better than howin' neeps or howkin' tatties!'

SOURCES

Adams, Norman (1993), *Hangman's Brae: Crime and Punishment in and around Bygone Aberdeen*, Banchory: Tolbooth Books.

Adams, Norman (1996), *Scotland's Chronicles of Blood*, London: Robert Hale.

Anderson, James (1843, revised 1879), *The Black Book of Kincardineshire*, Aberdeen: Lewis Smith.

Anderson, Robert (1910), *Aberdeen in Bygone Days*, Aberdeen: Aberdeen Daily Journal.

Birnie, Helen M. and Sheila M. Jessiman (2000), *St Fergus Past and Present*, St Fergus: St Fergus Community Press.

Carnie, William (1902–06), *Reporting Reminiscences*, Aberdeen: AUP.

Chambers, Robert (1980), *Traditions of Edinburgh*, Edinburgh: W. & R. Chambers.

Cockburn, Lord (1888), *Circuit Journeys*, Edinburgh: David Douglas.

Cramond, William (1880), *Annals of Cullen*, Banff: Banffshire Journal.

Dickinson, W. C. (1957), *Early Records of the Burgh of Aberdeen, 1398–1407*, Edinburgh: Scottish History Society.

Ferguson, Keith (1995), *The Black Kalendar of Aberdeen, 1746–1878*, Aberdeen: Aberdeen and North-East Scotland Family History Society.

Fraser, G. M. and Moira Henderson (1911), *Aberdeen Street Names* (updated James G. Bisset, 1986), Aberdeen.

Fraser, G. M. (1905), *Historical Aberdeen*, Aberdeen: The Bon-Accord Press.

Grant, James (1887), *Old and New Edinburgh*, London: Cassell & Co.

Hobbs, Alexander (1973–74), *Downie's Slaughter*, Aberdeen: Aberdeen University Review.

Irvine, Hamish (1972), *The Diced Cap, The Story of Aberdeen City Police*, Aberdeen: Aberdeen City Corporation.

Keith, Alexander (1972), *A Thousand Years of Aberdeen*, Aberdeen: Aberdeen University Press.

Keith, Alexander (1984), *Eminent Aberdonians*, Aberdeen: Aberdeen Chamber of Commerce.

Kennedy, William (1818), *Annals of Aberdeen*. Aberdeen: A. Brown & Co.

Lowson, Alexander (1891), *Tales, Legends and Traditions of Forfarshire*, Forfar: John MacDonald.

Lumsden, Louisa Innes (1927), *Memories of Aberdeen a Hundred Years Ago* (reprinted 1988 by Keith Murray (Aberdeen)), Aberdeen: Bon Accord Press.

McPherson, J. M. (1929), *Primitive Beliefs in the North-east of Scotland*, London: Longmans.

Mackinnon, Lachlan (1935), *Recollections of an Old Lawyer*, Aberdeen: D. Wyllie & Son.

Miller, Joyce (2004), *Magic and Witchcraft in Scotland*, Musselburgh: Goblinshead.

Millar, A. H. (1884), *The Black Kalendar of Scotland: Records of Notable Scottish Trials*, Dundee: John Leng & Co.

Milne, John (1911), *Aberdeen*, Aberdeen: Aberdeen Journal.

Morgan, Diane (1993), *The Villages of Aberdeen: Footdee and her Shipyards*, Aberdeen: Denburn Books.

Munro, Alexander (vol. 1 – 1899, vol. 5 – 1909), *Records of Old Aberdeen*, Aberdeen: New Spalding Club.

Rettie, James (1868), *Aberdeen Fifty Years Ago*, Aberdeen: Lewis Smith.

Robbie, William (1893), *Aberdeen: Traditions and History*, Aberdeen: D. Wyllie & Son.

Robertson, Joseph (1839), *The Book of Bon-Accord*, Aberdeen: Lewis Smith.

Roughead, William (1913), *Twelve Scots Trials*, Edinburgh: William Green & Sons.

Roughead, William (1935), *Knaves' Looking Glass*, London: Cassell & Co, 1935.

Roughead, William (1936), *In Queer Street*, Edinburgh: William Green & Sons.

Sillett, S. W. (1970), *Illicit Scotch*, Aberdeen: Impulse.

Skelton, Douglas (2004), *Indian Peter: The Extraordinary Life and Adventures of Peter Williamson*, Edinburgh: Mainstream.

Skene, William (1905), *East Neuk Chronicles*, Aberdeen: Aberdeen Journal.

Smith, Lewis (1807–10), *Autographic Notes and Comments 1807–80* (unpublished).

Spender, J. A. (1930), *Weetman Pearson, First Viscount Cowdray*, London: Cassell.

Stuart, John (1841, 1852), *The Miscellany of the Spalding Club*, vols I (1841) and V (1852), Aberdeen: W. Bennett.

Thom, Walter (1811), *History of Aberdeen*, Aberdeen: D. Chalmers & Co.

Turreff, Gavin (1859), *Antiquarian Gleanings from Aberdeenshire Records*, Aberdeen: James Murray.

Watt, Archibald (undated), *Highways and Byways Round Stonehaven*, Aberdeen: The Waverley Press.

Watt, Archibald (1985), *Highways and Byways Round Kincardine*, Aberdeen: Gordoun House.

Webster, George (1880), *Criminal Officer of the Old School*, Aberdeen, printed privately.

Webster, Paul (2000), *The Bridewell Prison: The story of Aberdeen's forgotten jail*, Aberdeen: Aberdeen and North-East Scotland Family History Society.

Whittington-Egan, Molly (2001), *The Stockbridge Baby Farmer and other Scottish Murders*, Glasgow: Neil Wilson.

Williamson, Peter (1878), *The Life and Curious Adventures of Peter Williamson, who was carried off from Aberdeen, in 1744, and sold for a slave etc.*, Aberdeen: James Daniel.

Wilson, Robert (1822), *The Book of Bon-Accord*, Aberdeen: Lewis Smith.

Wyness, Fenton (1965), *City by the Grey North Sea: Aberdeen*, Aberdeen: Alex P. Reid.

Young, Alex F. (1998), *The Encyclopaedia of Scottish Executions, 1750–1963*, Orpington: Eric Dobby.

The Black Kalendar of Aberdeen (four editions were published by various Aberdeen printing houses, the last by James Daniel & Son in 1878).

A Report of the Trial of Malcolm Gillespie and George Skene Edwards for Forgery (1827), Aberdeen: William Robertson.

The Tolbooth, Aberdeen's Museum of Civic History (1995), Aberdeen: Aberdeen City Council.

The Trial of Margaret Tindal alias Shuttleworth, for the Murder of her husband, Henry Shuttleworth etc. (1821), Montrose: John Smith.

Aberdeen Journal Notes and Queries (vol. III, 1910).

The Life and Remarkable Adventures of Peter Young, the Famous Caird (1867), Aberdeen.

In course of his research, the author also consulted the following publications:

Aberdeen Chronicle, Aberdeen Daily Free Press, Aberdeen Evening Express (1881–99), *Aberdeen Free Press and Buchan News, Aberdeen Herald, Aberdeen Journal, Aberdeen Leopard, Aberdeen Observer, Blackwood's Edinburgh Magazine* (May 1848), *The Deeside Field* (1931), *Elgin Courant, The Illustrated London News* (1881) and *Inverness Journal*.

INDEX